Hardwood Floors

Hardwood Floors

Laying, sanding and finishing

DON BOLLINGER

The Taunton Press

Cover photo: Roger Turk
Frontispiece: Bruce Greenlaw
Text photos: Roger Turk, except where noted

The Taunton Press
Inspiration for hands-on living®

20 19 18 17 16 15 14 13 12 11 10
Printed in the United States of America

A FINE HOMEBUILDING Book
FINE HOMEBUILDING® is a trademark of The Taunton Press,
Inc., registered in the U.S. Patent and Trademark Office.

The Taunton Press, 63 South Main Street, Box 5506,
Newtown, CT 06470-5506
e-mail: tp@taunton.com

Distributed by Publishers Group West

Library of Congress Cataloging-in-Publication Data

Bollinger, Don.
    Hardwood floors : laying, sanding and finishing /
Don Bollinger.
        p.   cm.
    "A Fine homebuilding book"—T.p. verso.
    ISBN 0-942391-62-4
    1. Floors, Wooden.   2. Hardwoods.   I. Title.
    TH2529.W6B65   1990
    694'.6 – dc20   90-11065
                                                CIP

To Jerry Hannan, an old friend, a good floor mechanic and a fine human being.

Contents

Introduction

Since the early 1980s, wood flooring has undergone a phenomenal resurgence in popularity, both for residential and commercial construction. To those of us in the flooring business, this comes as no surprise; for even though other materials may be cheaper or faster to install, wood retains a beauty, warmth and durability that's hard to match.

In one form or another, wood flooring has been afoot for centuries but in some ways, it's just now in its heyday. Because home buyers have become discerning enough to insist on wood flooring, the companies that make it have introduced flooring in unprecedented variety. As recently as a decade ago, oak strip flooring was the standard, if rather limited, fare. Today, you can buy flooring in dozens of species, and not just strip flooring, either, but in the wide planks once found only in well-preserved period homes. If you can't find the strip or plank flooring to suit you, it's a simple matter to have flooring made to order. Parquet flooring, which was hard to come by during the 1960s, is once again available in wide variety. Along with the flooring have come new finishes that are faster to apply and more durable than the coatings they replace.

All of this means that it's now more practical than ever for the owner-builder to install a new floor or to refurbish an old one. Note that I said "practical" and not "easy." I don't for an instant pretend that flooring is easy. Carting bundles of flooring up a flight of stairs, puzzling out a layout and nailing the floor down are all physically and mentally demanding tasks. It's not the sort of thing you can rush into and expect good results. Nonetheless, laying a wood floor is well within the ability of anyone with average tool dexterity. It takes very few special tools, materials are readily available and, if this book does its job, the skills will come quickly.

I've intentionally limited the breadth of this book to three major kinds of wood flooring: strip, plank and parquet. Through drawings, photos and text, I have attempted to explain as thoroughly as possible how to install each kind of flooring. However, I have by no means covered every variation of each type, preferring instead to convey enough fundamentals to allow you to interpolate solutions for problems not specifically discussed. Like any other trade, flooring has its share of "special cases"— what to do, for example, when new flooring must match old or how to deal with radiant heating. I've tried to include real-world solutions to these problems, but again, not every situation is covered.

As are all endeavors, this book is a bit of a compromise. I have written it primarily with the experienced owner-builder in mind, so most of the book is devoted to detailed how-to information on installing wood floors. However, readers who wish to subcontract the work to a professional will also find useful information, especially in Chapter 1, which deals with selecting and specifying floors, and in Chapter 2, which explains material grading rules. These chapters should also be informative to architects, designers and builders who may occasionally need to deal with flooring contractors. And although I don't intend this book as a trade manual, I hope professional floor mechanics will find useful nuggets within its pages.

With a little extra attention and work, a hardwood floor can elevate an ordinary room to the spectacular.

Why Install a Wood Floor?

Chapter 1

Back in the early 1930s, when the Farmer's Home Administration began issuing cheap mortgages, it required all houses to have hardwood floors. In those days, before the broadloom made wall-to-wall carpet affordable, a hardwood floor was considered a necessity for civilized living. The FHA stopped requiring hardwood floors some time ago, but wood flooring still retains its reputation for quality and durability.

Traditionally, wood flooring was found throughout the house. Now it tends to be concentrated in heavy traffic areas like halls or foyers or in rooms such as the kitchen, where frequent cleaning rules out other materials. It's true that a wood floor will outlast your mortgage and retain its beauty long after carpet or vinyl has been replaced. But the best reason for installing a wood floor is that, dollar for dollar, no other material matches wood's aesthetic versatility and practicality. Depending on the style, species and finish, wood suits virtually any architectural or decorative style.

That's not to suggest that wood is cheap. In cost, it ranks somewhere between carpet and tile. Because it has to be installed piece by piece and then sanded and finished, a wood floor is very labor intensive. If you have a contractor install your floor, expect to pay for that labor. Even if you do the work yourself—and this book is intended to show you how—a wood floor will cost you plenty of sweat. If you're laying and site-finishing hardwood in an average-size living room and dining room, expect to put up with the mess of installation for the better part of two weeks. In the long run, though, that labor pays off nicely, because most solid-wood floors can be renewed many times with sanding and refinishing.

Bollinger's signature decorative touch is brass and ebony inlaid around borders.

This is the oak strip floor the author installed to illustrate this book and the accompanying videotape.

Where a wood floor works best

As I said earlier, wood floors are well suited to rooms exposed to heavy foot traffic or frequent cleaning. These include entry halls, reception areas, kitchens, powder rooms, hallways, dens and playrooms. Living rooms, dining rooms and formal parlors are good candidates for wood flooring too. Although these rooms don't always get a lot of traffic, an appealing floor design, perhaps variable-width planking or parquet, will give them a unique atmosphere that's just right for an occasional room.

Sometimes a wood floor can solve a design or structural problem. For example, strip flooring nailed firmly to the subfloor and joists can actually strengthen a marginal floor system so you end up with a firmer, quieter walking surface. A wood strip floor is really a floor, not just a floor covering, like carpet or vinyl.

Rooms that would otherwise appear cold—aesthetically and thermally—can be warmed up by a wood floor. These days, wood floors are available in dozens of species, each with its own grain and color. Moreover, as I'll explain later, there are three distinct styles of wood flooring to choose from, and a range of choices within each style.

Wood is an excellent insulator. One inch of wood has the same insulating value as 15 in. of concrete; if you want to improve the R-value, it's sometimes possible to

Strip and plank are common forms of wood flooring. Oak strip (above) is sold in a wide range of widths, grades, species and sizes. On this floor, an inexpensive grade of short strips produces an appealing pattern. Once found only where strip flooring wasn't available, plank flooring (right) has become increasingly popular. Like strip, it's sold both finished and unfinished and in a number of species and widths.

install thin foam insulation and a moisture barrier underneath a wood floor. For those who insist that wood flooring is cold to the feet, a wood floor works nicely over radiant heat.

Despite my enthusiasm for wood floors, they aren't suitable for every room in the house, regardless of what the foot traffic may suggest. Wood flooring in a room that's exposed directly to the elements or excessive moisture will be nothing but trouble. I don't recommend solid wood for basement floors or in below-grade, high-moisture areas, although in some circumstances, laminated flooring is suitable. That's not to say that I won't install wood below grade; I just won't guarantee it.

Leaky appliances, weeping flower pots and other sources of constant moisture will discolor and eventually destroy a floor. Similarly, constant bright sunshine will eventually degrade the finish and topmost layers of the wood, requiring premature sanding and refinishing. Later in this book, I'll explain how to compensate for seasonal moisture changes when flooring is installed. But wild swings in humidity and liquid water are more than most wood floors can handle.

Wood versus other materials

In helping clients decide on a wood floors, I start by comparing wood to other kinds of flooring. Assuming the room is suitable for wood in the first place, other possibilities include carpeting, resilient flooring (vinyl sheet and tile) and ceramic tile. Marble is also a choice, but it's very similar to ceramic tile so I lump them together.

First of all, let's consider durability. With reasonable care, wood will outlast carpet and vinyl several times over. True, it may need refinishing once, twice or even three times during its life, but at minimum, a wood floor ought to last 20 years. It's not uncommon to find perfectly serviceable 100-year-old wood floors.

High-quality carpeting is tough stuff, too, but depending on the foot traffic, it begins to look threadbare after 20 years and may deteriorate a lot sooner than that. Even cheap replacement carpeting will cost more than a refinishing job on a hardwood floor. Ceramic tile is probably more durable than wood, but a hard object dropped on a tile floor will break a tile, calling for a tricky repair. A dropped object will probably make a repairable dent in a wood floor but, with any luck, what you dropped on it won't break.

Although considered expensive by many, some parquet flooring is actually cheaper than many kinds of strip and plank. Two styles are shown, a pattern floor made of short pieces of strip flooring (above) and Canterbury parquet (below).

Day-to-day care of a wood floor involves sweeping or damp mopping. Unlike carpeting, which acts like a giant rag, wood won't collect molds and mildew or absorb dust. This delights anyone with allergies. It takes longer to vacuum a carpet than hard surface flooring, and vacuuming never does a thorough job. Even professional cleaning removes only a fraction of the dirt, mold and fungus growing there. Depending on the material and color, tile floors can be very difficult to keep tidy. Some require periodic treatments with sealer to keep them clean.

On the down side, some wood floors require occasional waxing, stripping and rewaxing and, of course, eventual sanding and refinishing. Some new flooring products are delivered prefinished with very durable, baked-on finishes. Some of these don't need waxing, but because they're not sanded after installation, they inevitably have "overwood," or minor thickness or height variations between pieces. A common way of disguising overwood is with chamfers or eased edges on each piece of flooring. Unfortunately, these create gaps between boards into which hard-to-remove dust and debris can lodge.

Although not as fire resistant and water resistant as tile, solid wood requires an extremely high temperature to burn. Should a wood floor ignite, it won't give off toxic fumes, like burning carpet or resilient flooring. Most modern finishes, particularly the Swedish finish I prefer, protect wood floors against damage from liquid water.

As for square-foot cost, wood costs more than carpeting or resilient flooring but is cheaper than tile. This depends, of course, on the style of flooring, the species of wood and the room where the installation will be done. Some wood floors, parquet over ¾-in. plywood sheathing, for example, will require underlayment, which adds to the cost. You have to factor finishing into the cost of a wood floor, too, unless you're using prefinished flooring. The chart below compares costs of common flooring materials.

Types of flooring

Hardwood flooring is sold in three major types: strip, plank and parquet. These days, all three types are likely to be available in considerable variety, both finished and unfinished. Strip flooring consists of narrow boards nailed side by side to the subfloor, and it's what most of us think of when we talk about oak floors. But plank flooring—essentially just like strip flooring, only wider—is making inroads into strip's dominance. Parquet (and wood block flooring) is made in individual tiles, often with a pattern, which are nailed or glued to the floor. In Seattle, where I install most of my floors, parquet flooring runs a distant third in popularity.

Even if your supplier doesn't stock it, strip and plank flooring are made in the widths and thicknesses shown. At left in the photo below are three widths of strip and four of plank, all side and end matched. At right is ⅜-in. thick strip flooring. The top two are tongue and groove; the bottom piece is square edged.

Flooring Costs Compared					
Floor type	Cost per sq. ft. to install	Labor as a percent of installed cost	Floor type	Cost per sq. ft. to install	Labor as a percent of installed cost
Residential carpet	$2.75 to $4.00	10% to 15%	Resilient flooring (vinyl, sheet and tile)	$1.50 to $8.00	10% to 15%
Commercial carpet	$4.00 to $9.00	10% to 15%			
Hardwood flooring	$4.50 to $10.00	50% to 60%	Thickset tile	$10.00 to $20.00	50% to 60%
Thinset tile	$6.00 to $12.00	40% to 50%	Marble or slate	$10.00 to $20.00	50% to 60%

Five parquet styles, clockwise from left: Canterbury, Monticello, Finger block and Haddon Hall; at center, Rhombus.

Strip flooring is pretty versatile stuff, making it a good choice for practically any application where a wood floor is wanted. Strip can be nailed to plywood or plank subfloors or to screeds over a concrete slab. It's sold in raw, unfinished wood or in prestained and prefinished stock that's ready to go as soon as it's nailed down.

Plank flooring. Plank flooring also comes square edged or side and end matched. It's available in 3-in., 4-in., 5-in. 6-in. and 7-in. widths but can be ordered in wider boards. Plank thicknesses typically range from $\frac{5}{16}$ in. to $1\frac{1}{2}$ in., though other thicknesses are sometimes available. Like strip flooring, plank is nailed to the subfloor, either through the tongues and grooves or through the face of the boards. Because of its width, plank is often screwed to the floor as well (the screw holes can be covered with wooden plugs that add a nice decorative touch).

Plank is suitable for any room in which strip might be installed. In the better grades, the wood is free of character marks and wild grain and because there are fewer, wider boards, the finished floor has a more homogeneous look than a strip floor in the same species. If face nailed or screwed and plugged, a plank floor has a rustic, informal look. In fact, several manufacturers have capitalized on this by making flooring from beams salvaged from old buildings. The aged wood has an appealing patina that gives a new floor a lived-in look.

Depending on the grade, plank flooring is slightly more expensive than strip. It's sold prefinished and unfinished. Figure 1 shows the various types of hardwood flooring.

Parquet flooring. Parquet is potentially the most spectacular of all the flooring types. In some ways, it has more in common with ceramic tile than with wood. Parquetry comes in individual tiles; the most common but by no means only sizes are 9x9, 11x11, 12x12 and 19x19. Each tile consists of a number of pieces arranged to form some sort of pattern. As the tiles themselves are laid, a larger, more complex pattern emerges. The photo at left shows a few of the common parquet patterns, but more are discussed in Chapter 2.

Parquet is usually $\frac{5}{16}$ in. or $\frac{3}{4}$ in. thick. Sometimes it's end matched with tongue and groove, but more often it's square edged. Quite often, regular $2\frac{1}{4}$-in. strip flooring is cut to fixed lengths and sold as parquet, the idea being to nail it down in a pattern. Technically, though, parquet flooring is sold in individual tiles.

Parquet can't be installed just anywhere. If you're not careful about it, a parquet floor's insistent pattern can be a nightmarish jumble of geometric patterns that clash with the walls or the furniture. In some rooms, say a kitchen, a low-key strip or plank would look just fine, but a parquet pattern would draw more attention to the floor than you might want. On the other hand, a nicely handled parquet floor can add an inviting formality to a dining room or living room.

Strip flooring. Although much of it is made of $2\frac{1}{4}$-in. wide oak, strip flooring actually comes in far greater variety than most people realize. Strip flooring is available in $\frac{3}{4}$-in., $1\frac{1}{2}$-in., $1\frac{3}{4}$-in., $2\frac{1}{4}$-in. and $2\frac{3}{4}$-in. widths. Thicknesses range from $\frac{5}{16}$ in. to $\frac{33}{32}$ in., though $\frac{3}{4}$ in. is by far the most common. As will be explained in Chapter 2, the flooring is sold in bundles of various lengths.

Most modern strip flooring is side and end matched, which means that both the long edges and the short ends of each piece are tongue and grooved. When fit tightly together and nailed firmly to the subfloor, the tongues and grooves make a stiff assembly that improves the structural integrity of the building. In older homes you'll sometimes see square-edged flooring, without tongues or grooves. Square-edged flooring is still available, but most people prefer side-and-end-matched flooring.

Figure 1 **Hardwood Flooring Types**

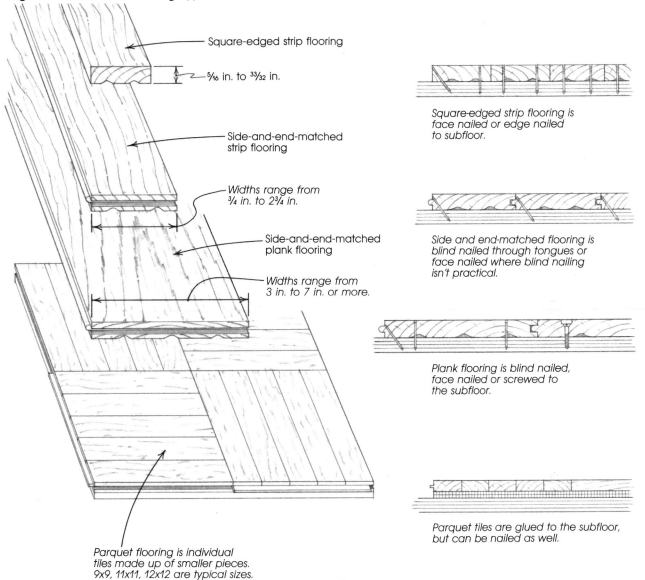

Square-edged strip flooring

5⁄16 in. to 33⁄32 in.

Side-and-end-matched strip flooring

Widths range from ¾ in. to 2¾ in.

Side-and-end-matched plank flooring

Widths range from 3 in. to 7 in. or more.

Square-edged strip flooring is face nailed or edge nailed to subfloor.

Side and end-matched flooring is blind nailed through tongues or face nailed where blind nailing isn't practical.

Plank flooring is blind nailed, face nailed or screwed to the subfloor.

Parquet tiles are glued to the subfloor, but can be nailed as well.

Parquet flooring is individual tiles made up of smaller pieces. 9x9, 11x11, 12x12 are typical sizes.

Thin parquet is generally glued to the subfloor, and ¾-in. material can be glued or nailed. Because the individual tiles add no strength to the floor, parquet requires a sounder subfloor than does strip or plank.

What happens when

One of the most vexing problems facing the amateur floor mechanic is not so much how to install a wood floor but when. It's the general contractor's job to keep a new house or remodel on schedule, so he's supposed to know when to call the drywall sub, when to get the painters

started and when to get the floors done. If you are planning on doing your own floors in a job that will be overseen by a general contractor, consult with the contractor about when to start.

Chances are, though, you'll be acting as your own general contractor, so the decision will be up to you. My best advice is to wait until near the last minute to install the floors. As I'll explain in Chapter 2, processes which release lots of moisture—the drywalling and painting of the walls with latex paint—wreak havoc with wood flooring, so these should definitely be done first.

Ideally, the trimwork, baseboards, doors casings and so on should be installed after the floor. This won't always

Although the work isn't easy, installing, sanding and finishing a hardwood floor should be well within the ability of anyone with average tool skills.

be possible, however. If the trim has to go on first, a conscientious trim carpenter will inquire about the kind of flooring to be installed so he can leave sufficient space between the bottom of the door casings and subfloor for the flooring to be slipped in. He'll also wait until the flooring is completed before installing the baseboard so there will be room to sand up to the wall edges.

If conflict comes, it'll probably be with the painter who wants to paint all of the trimwork before the floor is sanded and finished. This is like painting a truck just before taking it four-wheeling. The lower part of the baseboard and casing will inevitably get banged up when the floor gets sanded. Just make sure the painter will come back at no additional charge to touch up the blemished trim.

How long will it take?

Like any building trade, flooring has enough surprises to make estimating a tricky business, especially the time that will be required to complete a job. A professional flooring mechanic is expected install between 300 and 400 sq. ft. of strip or plank in an eight-hour day and about 400 sq. ft. of parquet.

Sanding an average floor, say 1,000 sq. ft., will take two to three days, and finishing will take another two to three days, depending on the type of finish and the weather. Add to that the time required for preparation, material handling and cleanup, and you can see that even a small floor will take the better part of a week to complete. If there's lots of detail work like cabinets, headers and borders, the job can take much longer.

Whether they are having it done by a contractor or doing it themselves, people tend to underestimate the time required to do a floor and the inevitable inconvenience and mess that go along with it. Flooring is a very intrusive process. Before I start a job, I give my customers a ten-page description of what they'll have to put up with. Here is a short list of what they'll have to do or have done: move and store the furniture; remove and possibly replace the baseboards; move and store knickknacks so they won't be jarred loose from shelves; mask off the house to prevent dust seepage; move the stove or clothes dryer to allow access to 220-volt receptacles; live with the strong odor of finishes for several days.

Of course, I'm quick to point out that the inconvenience is more than worth it since the reward is a beautiful hardwood floor that will last for years to come.

Since the mid-1970s, when wood flooring came back into vogue, strip flooring and plank flooring have become available in unprecedented variety.

Materials, Estimating and Tools

Chapter 2

Because much of the hardwood flooring that I sell is bought by weekend do-it-yourselfers, I teach an occasional evening class on how to install, sand and finish flooring. As I explain in the class, laying a floor is relatively simple once you've grasped the basic principles. Figuring out what kind of flooring meets your needs is not so simple.

These days, there are so many kinds of flooring that you could spend a day in a retail showroom and still not see it all. In oak strip flooring alone you'll be confronted with a half-dozen different widths, two or three thicknesses and four grades. If that's not enough to think about, the grades are different for other species and are sometimes different within the same species if the flooring is sold both finished and unfinished.

In some ways the flooring business is like the fashion industry. Every season brings some new style and products seem to come and go, depending on what species are available and what the public's taste happens to be. There are regional favorites, too. In San Francisco, for example, square-edged face-nailed strip flooring is popular in the restored Victorian houses the city is known for. On the East Coast and in the Southeast, plank flooring in indigenous yellow or heart pine is a favorite.

Generally speaking, though, the old standbys—common widths of oak strip and plank and popular parquet patterns—don't change much. Except for variations in price, what you can buy here in Seattle you can also buy in St. Louis or Baltimore. In this chapter, I'll describe the basic types, grades and species of flooring. Keep in mind, however, that some of the specialty flooring I'll mention here will not be available locally or may have passed out of fashion by the time you read this book.

Where flooring comes from

A hundred years ago, the flooring business was a cottage industry. Flooring mills were located near both the source of raw materials and the market. Manufacturing standards were mostly non-existent or loosely observed. The railroads (and later trucks) changed the picture drastically, so that today, oak flooring from Tennessee is routinely shipped to California, just as Oregon fir finds its way to the Northeast.

Flooring mills turn out flooring by the lineal mile, one piece at a time. The strips are ripped, thicknessed and then tongued and grooved.

Flooring manufacture is still regional in the sense that mills are generally located near their sources of supply. However, there are two trade associations that have established grading rules and manufacturing standards that apply to most of the mills in the United States. The bigger of these is the National Oak Flooring Manufacturer's Association (NOFMA), to which about 80% of the country's oak flooring manufacturers belong. NOFMA publishes (and enforces) grading rules and standards for oak, beech, birch, maple and pecan flooring. The Maple Flooring Manufacturers Association (MFMA) oversees production of maple flooring.

By inspecting the mills and their products, the trade associations are supposed to ensure that grading rules are met, and by and large, they do. The associations also investigate complaints from distributors or customers. However, just because a bundle of flooring bears the NOFMA or MFMA stamp, it doesn't necessarily mean that it won't contain misgraded or shoddily milled pieces. On the other hand, flooring produced by non-association mills will probably conform to the grading rules and may be made to the same or even better standards. I've used flooring from association and non-association manufacturers with equal success because I always make it a point to know my supplier before purchasing. If you're buying blind, I'd suggest that you make sure the flooring has a trade-association stamp. For the addresses of the associations, see the Resource Guide on p. 135.

In Chapter 1, I described the three major kinds of flooring and offered some suggestions on how you might decide which kind to install. So far, so good. Once you've settled on the flooring type, though, you still have to figure out sizes, species, grade, patterns and whether or not you want finished or unfinished material. For strip or plank flooring, you'll also have to specify how you want the flooring bundled.

Strip flooring

Because it's the most popular kind of flooring, strip is generally available in more variety than any other type. Practically every neighborhood lumberyard has bundles of 2¼-in. end-matched flooring lying around. But just because they sell it, it doesn't mean you should buy it there. If there's one thing I'm certain of, it's that wood flooring can't be handled and stored like studs and plywood. It has to be stored in a dry (preferably heated) shed by people who know flooring materials.

Solid-wood strip flooring can be bought in ¾-in., 1½-in., 1¾-in., 2¼-in. and 2¾-in. widths and in thicknesses from ⁵⁄₁₆ in. to 1½ in. Which width and thickness you choose depends on the look you're after. Narrow strip tends to make the floor look busy, especially in the lower grades, where there's lots of grain variation. It's also more labor intensive since more nailing is required for a given

After milling, strip flooring is sorted and bundled by size, grade and species.

Trade associations like the National Oak Flooring Manufacturers Association police grading rules. Member mills stamp their products with a logo, like the one shown here.

floor size. Conversely, wider flooring in the better grades will appear to be more of a single piece because the figure is subdued and even. The wider the flooring, the more you can expect to pay, given the equivalent grade.

As for thickness, ¾ in. is the usual choice for unfinished strip flooring. In circumstances where the height gain of ¾-in. flooring can't be tolerated for some reason, you might elect to use thinner flooring. But the thinner the flooring, the less you'll be able to sand it when it's time to refinish. For the same reason, flooring that is thicker than ¾ in. will stand up to more sanding and refinishing, but the material will have to be special ordered and is likely to be expensive.

Strip flooring is normally side and end matched, with tongues and grooves along the edges and in the ends. It's possible to buy either square edged (no tongue and groove) or side matched (tongue and groove only on the edges), but I prefer to work with side-and-end-matched flooring. It's a little easier to install and usually makes a stronger floor because the combination of edge and end tongues lock the floor into a single, rigid unit. Where side-and-end-matched flooring can be quickly nailed through the tongues, square-edged flooring has to be painstakingly face nailed. Face nails have to be set and the holes filled before sanding and finishing—this is a lot of extra work.

Hardwood flooring grades. My customers have a lot of questions about how their flooring will look when it's installed. This is always difficult to communicate because everyone has a different perception of color and grain pattern. I often answer by comparing cabinet-grade wood with flooring. In a typical oak cabinet you're looking at wood from three or four different trees, but in an oak floor the boards are taken from dozens of trees, many of which may be from different parts of the same forest or even a different region.

If you've ever picked through a stack of oak boards, you've probably discovered that no two are identical. Most of the variation is in color and figure and what floormen call "character marks," the pin knots, swirls, ray tissue, dark spots and so on that comprise what laymen consider "grain." Grading rules published by NOFMA and the other trade groups are an attempt to sort boards into categories of *like variation.* That's not to say the boards will be identical (they won't be). But the variations will be predictable enough to appear harmonious. You don't have to become an expert on grading rules, but you'll need some knowledge of them in order to purchase flooring intelligently.

The chart on p. 18 describes the NOFMA grading rules for unfinished oak, maple, beech and birch strip and plank flooring and for prefinished oak. Other species,

Grading Chart: National Oak Flooring Manufacturers Association

Unfinished oak flooring	Unfinished hard maple, beech and birch flooring	Unfinished pecan flooring	Prefinished oak flooring	Prefinished beech and pecan flooring

Unfinished oak flooring

Clear plainsawn or clear quartersawn

Best appearance, most uniform color, limited small character marks. Bundles 1¼ ft. and up, average length 3¾ ft.

Select plainsawn or select quartersawn

Excellent appearance, limited character marks, unlimited sound sapwood. Bundles 1¼ ft. and up, average length 3¼ ft.

Select and better is a combination of clear and select grades.

No. 1 Common

Variegated appearance, knots, worm holes and other marks allowed to provide variegated appearance after filling. Bundles 1¼ ft. and up, average length 2¾ ft.

No. 2 Common

Rustic appearance with all characteristics of species, serviceable after defects have been filled; red and white oak may be mixed. Bundles 1¼ ft. and up, average length 2¼ ft.

Shorts grades

114 Shorts

Pieces 9 in. to 18 in. long, bundles average 1¼ ft.

No. 1 Common and better shorts

Combination of clear, select and No. 1 Common.

No. 2 Common shorts

Same as No. 2 Common.

Unfinished hard maple, beech and birch flooring

First grade

Best appearance, natural color variation, limited character marks, unlimited sapwood. Bundles 2 ft. and up; 2-ft. and 3-ft. bundles comprise 33% of total footage.

First-grade white hard maple, beech and birch are custom order only.

Second grade

Variegated appearance, varying sound wood characterics of species. Bundles 2 ft. and up; 2-ft. and 3-ft. bundles comprise 45% of footage.

Second and better grade

A combination of first and second grades. Bundles 2 ft. and up; 2-ft. and 3-ft. bundles comprise up to 40% of footage.

Third grade

Rustic appearance, all characteristics of species, serviceable after defects have been filled. Bundles 1¼ ft. and up; 1¼-ft. to 3-ft. bundles comprise 65% of footage.

Third and better grade

A combination of second and third grades, bundles 1¼ and up; 1¼-ft. to 3-ft. bundles comprise 50% of footage.

Unfinished pecan flooring

First grade

Excellent appearance, natural color variation, limited character marks, unlimited sapwood. Bundles 2 ft. and up; 2-ft. and 3-ft. bundles comprise up to 25% of footage.

First-grade red and white pecan are custom orders.

Second grade

Variegated appearance, varying sound wood characteristics of species. Bundles 1¼ ft. and up; 1¼-ft. to 3-ft. bundles comprise 40% of footage.

Second and better grade

A combination of first and second grades.

Third grade

Rustic appearance, all wood characteristics of species, serviceable after filling. Bundles 1¼ ft. and up; 1¼-ft. to 3-ft. bundles comprise 60% of footage.

Third and better grade

A combination of first, second and third grades.

Prefinished oak flooring

Prime grade (special order)

Excellent appearance, natural color variation, limited character marks, unlimited sapwood. Bundles 1¼ ft. and up, average length 3½ ft.

Standard grade

Variegated appearance, varying sound wood characteristics of species. Bundles 1¼ ft. and up, average length 2¾ ft.

Standard and better grade

Combination of standard and prime. Bundles 1¼ ft. and up, average length 3 ft.

Tavern grade

Rustic appearance, all characteristics of species. Bundles 1¼ ft. and up, average length 2¼ ft.

Tavern and better grade

Combination of prime, standard and tavern.

Prefinished beech and pecan flooring

Tavern and better grade

Combination of prime, standard and tavern grades, all wood characteristics of species. Bundles to 1¼ ft. and up, average length 3 ft.

Oak flooring grades shown.

Clear

Select

No. 1 Common

No. 2 Common

Side-and-end-matched strip flooring: sizes

Standard	Special order	Square edged	Plank
¾ x 2¼	¾ x 2	⁵⁄₁₆ x 2	¾ x 3, 4, 5, 6, 7, 8
¾ x 1½	¹¹⁄₃₂ x 2	⁵⁄₁₆ x 1½	
¹⁵⁄₃₂ x 2	¹¹⁄₃₂ x 1½		
¹⁵⁄₃₂ x 1½			

Chart and photos courtesy of National Oak Floor Manufacturers Association.

Grading Chart: Maple Flooring Manufacturers Association		
First grade	**Second and better grade**	**Third grade**
Face practically defect free, strips 2 ft. to 8 ft. 20% of bundles 2 ft., not more than 45% under 4 ft.	Allows tight knots and slight imperfections, strip lengths 1¼ to 8 ft., not over 53% of total footage. Bundles under 4 ft., not more than 22% in 1¼-ft. bundles.	Strip lengths 1¼ to 8 ft., not more than 75% of total footage in bundles under 4 ft. and not more than 40% of total footage in 1¼-ft. bundles.

Chart courtesy of Maple Flooring Manufacturers Association.

mainly the softwoods and laminated products, have their own grading rules. Each set of rules has its own peculiarities. With the exception of maple, which is graded by both NOFMA and the Maple Flooring Manufacturing Association), there isn't any overlap. (The MFMA rules for maple are shown in the chart above.) Species that are rarely used for flooring, particularly the exotics, are not covered by any grading rules.

The charts may make grading appear more complicated than it really is, so I suggest you compare the photos of the four major grades of oak with the chart description. Note that the top two grades are lumped together under "Select and better." What this means is that you can order a mixture of the top two grades—Select and better—or you can specify the top grade or the next best grade—Select plain or quartersawn. Note too that the top grades can be specified in either quartersawn or plainsawn stock. Figure 2 shows the difference.

If you specify quartersawn, expect to special order it at premium prices, if you can get it at all. The chart on p. 20 gives some general information on flooring prices. However, flooring is a commodity, so prices are subject to practically daily change. The price relationships, though, should be relatively stable.

Figure 2 **Quartersawn vs. Plainsawn**

Plainsawn board

Quartersawn board

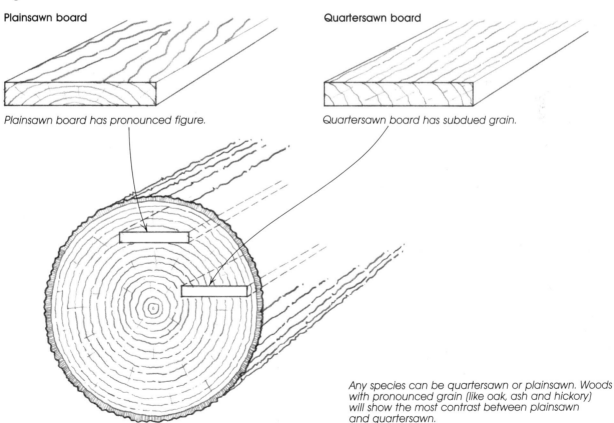

Plainsawn board has pronounced figure.

Quartersawn board has subdued grain.

Any species can be quartersawn or plainsawn. Woods with pronounced grain (like oak, ash and hickory) will show the most contrast between plainsawn and quartersawn.

Price Comparison: Typical Oak Grades*			
Grade	Retail price per foot	Grade	Retail price per foot
Clear quartersawn	$4.00	Select and better, plainsawn	3.00
Select quartersawn	$4.00	Select	$2.75
No. 1 quartersawn	$3.50 to $3.75	No. 1 Better	$2.25 to $2.50
Clear plainsawn	$3.25 to $3.50	No. 2 Common	$1.75

*Prices vary with season and locale.

Strip flooring is available in three kinds of bundles: random length, or average length; nested; and specified length. At left are average-length shorts bundles; below are 8-ft. long nested bundles.

Which flooring grade is best for you? Most of my customers decide to use Select and better because it represents a good compromise between cost and appearance. Select and better floors are fairly even in color and have very few knots and small character marks. Personally, I prefer No. 1 Common. It's got a lot of color and grain variation, as well as bold character marks that conform to what I think wood should look like. No. 2 Common makes a good utility floor for a back room, a shop or any area where you want a wood floor but where appearance isn't paramount.

Bundles. Strip flooring comes in bundles, sorted by both grade and length. Three kinds of bundles are available: random or average length; nested bundles; specified-length bundles. Regardless of the bundling method, the flooring in each bundle should accurately represent the grade it's supposed to be. Because grading is subjective, you might occasionally find a No. 1 Common board in a Select and better bundle, but generally the grades are as advertised. Bundles are usually stacked four strips deep and three strips wide. As explained on pp. 29-30, this makes figuring square footage relatively easy.

Random-length (or average-length) bundles are the most common. These contain strips of various lengths up to 8 ft., but no shorter than 9 in. The bundles are sold in nominal lengths from "shorts" to 8 ft. Except for shorts, each bundle may include pieces from 6 in. over to 6 in. under the bundle's nominal length. Short pieces (between 9 in. and 18 in.) are packaged together and are generally referred to as shorts. Every grade will contain some shorts. Generally, the lower the grade, the more shorts it will have in each bundle. Pieces 6 in. to 8 in. or 4 in. to 6 in., which I call mini-shorts and maxi-shorts respectively, are sometimes sold separately. These bits and pieces, left over from the milling process, are too short to go into random-length or nested bundles.

Nested bundles consist of random lengths sorted and bundled continuously to lengths of 6 ft. to 8 ft. The principal advantage of nested bundles is that you can more accurately figure the area that a given bundle will cover. Nested bundles are more uniform than random-length bundles, so less time is spent "racking," or sorting the pieces to avoid bad end matches.

Strip flooring can be bought in specified lengths. Usually, specified lengths are 2 ft. or less for pattern floors. A well-stocked flooring supplier will probably have random-length bundles in several grades, plus shorts of various sizes and perhaps nested bundles. Don't be surprised, though, if anything other than random length has to be special ordered.

Plank flooring

Any flooring 3 in. or wider is considered plank. Plank is widely sold in 1-in. increments from 3 in. up to 7 in., but wider boards are sometimes available. As with strip, plank is often side and end matched so it's blind nailed to the subfloor and/or face nailed and screwed. Plank flooring is available in hardwoods, but not as widely as it is in the softwoods—chiefly fir, hemlock and pine. Some companies specialize in exotic imported species; these may or may not conform to standard sizes but probably won't adhere to the grading rules. Several companies make flooring from the siding and structural beams of old wood buildings. These products are aimed at the restoration market and may or may not conform to the grades. Check with the supplier and ask to see a sample.

Plank flooring is sold in various thicknesses from 3/8 in. to 1 1/2 in. The thinner stock is often laminated and prefinished, although thicker laminated products are available. In the West, 2x6 tongue-and-groove plank flooring, often called car decking, is used as a structural subfloor, but it's not of a good enough grade for anything other than a utility finished floor. Car decking sometimes has a V-grooved edge that can be left exposed underneath to form the ceiling for the room below.

Selection criteria for grades of plank flooring are largely the same as strip and are described in the chart on p. 18. Plank flooring is boxed rather than bundled. Most mills seem to pack boxes as nested bundles. These boxes contain some shorts but there is no standard shorts grouping (as in strip) probably because short, wide boards appear to be too square and it's much harder to achieve staggered end matches with short pieces.

Individual pieces of parquet tiles are held together by plastic gauze on the back (at left) or paper facing (at right). A third method (not shown) consists of a soft metal spline threaded through the tiles.

Parquet flooring

Wood flooring in general has enjoyed a phenomenal resurgence during the past decade, but the popularity of parquet floors has been uneven, at best. I'm not really sure why this is so, because parquet is a good value and for the do-it-yourselfer, a parquet floor is relatively easy to install. Some people are under the mistaken assumption that because parquet is thinner, it's less durable than a strip or plank floor. Actually, a $^5/_{16}$-in. square-edged parquet floor has as much sandable wood as a $^3/_4$-in. strip floor, whose tongues and grooves will be exposed when $^1/_4$ in. of wood has been sanded away.

Parquet is considered to be any kind of floor with a repeating geometric pattern. The pattern can be formed right on the floor by nailing down short strips, or it can consist of individual parquet tiles made up of many small pieces arranged in a decorative pattern. To hold the tiles together during handling and installation, the pieces are loosely bonded to a paper, cloth or plastic mesh backing or stitched together by a thin, soft metal or plastic spline threaded through a groove.

Parquet tiles are installed by gluing them individually to the subfloor or, if they are thick enough, by face, edge or blind nailing. Some parquet even has peel-off adhesive already attached to a foam backing that provides thermal and sound insulation.

Standard parquet thicknesses are $^5/_{16}$ in. and $^3/_4$ in. Common tiles sizes are 9x9, 11x11, 12x12 and 19x19. The size and pattern are, of course, a matter of personal preference. Unless the pattern my client wants is available only in $^9/_{16}$ in. or $^3/_4$ in., I'll use $^5/_{16}$ in. Parquet in general is a good choice where moisture is liable to be a problem, because there's no consistent cross-grain expansion. Thin parquet is even better, because it expands less forcefully than thicker wood.

Figure 3 shows some of the traditional parquet patterns, but this is far from a complete representation. I've taken these samples from several catalogs just to give you some idea of what's available. A word of warning: There are few grading standards for parquet. Pattern styles and names change from one manufacturer to the next—one mill's Mt. Vernon might be another's Swirl. Make sure that you see a sample of the parquet you want from the company you'll be buying it from. Buy enough flooring to complete the job (plus a little extra) so you won't run into problems with variation between lots. And believe me, there will be lots of variation.

Figure 3 **Typical Parquet Patterns**

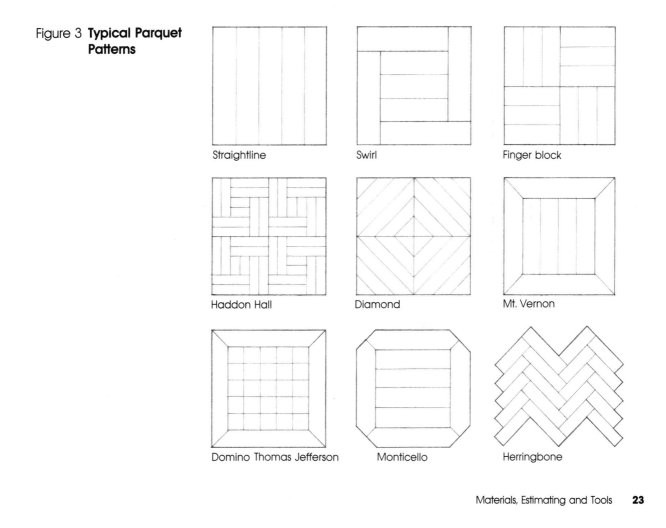

Straightline

Swirl

Finger block

Haddon Hall

Diamond

Mt. Vernon

Domino Thomas Jefferson

Monticello

Herringbone

Prefinished flooring, usually sold in nested bundles, is available in strip, plank and parquet. Prefinished products are available in both solid and laminated styles.

Most parquet made of oak is manufactured in the United States. If you canvass a few suppliers, however, you'll be able to locate walnut parquet and special order other species. Most common patterns can be found in teak, rosewood and other exotic species. If you are looking for something really exotic, you can special order your own pattern in any species from one of the suppliers listed in the Resource Guide on p. 134. Bring a blank check and hide your eyes, though. If you have to ask how much the bill will be, you can't afford it.

Laminated and prefinished products. By far the most difficult part of floor work is sanding and finishing. It's backbreaking, dusty work with a heavy machine that can wreak havoc in a moment of inattention. Unfortunately, there's no way to practice sanding. If you've never done it, you have to dive in and hope for the best. Once the dust is all swept up, the new floor is off limits for several odor-filled days while the finish dries. It's easy to see why hardwood flooring was a hard sell to do-it-yourselfers, and why prefinished products have such appeal.

Prefinished flooring was developed quite a while ago but came into its own during the mid-1970s, when very few professional floor finishers were to be found. It comes straight from the factory with stain and a very durable finish already applied. All you have to do is nail it down, sweep up a little sawdust and you're done. Prefinished flooring is blind nailed or glued to the subfloor. Where it must be face nailed, the nails are set and the holes filled with a colored wax that matches the finish. At it ages, a solid-wood prefinished floor can be sanded and refinished, just like a conventional floor.

It should come as no surprise that prefinished flooring is very popular. It accounts for about 15% or my contracting business and about 40% of my do-it-yourself sales. Most manufacturers offer strip, plank and parquet in some kind of prefinished grade. The grades are described in the chart on p. 18.

Besides eliminating sanding and finishing, prefinished flooring tends to have a tougher finish and a more even color. Factory finishing suffers from none of the constraints placed on the on-site finisher, so some rather exotic surface treatments are possible, including distressing, decorative pegs, coloring and very durable urethane or baked-on waxes.

One of the more elaborate methods of prefinishing involves impregnating the wood grain with an acrylic plastic finish. Although limited to relatively porous red oak in thin pieces, this process ensures absolutely even color through and through. Acrylic-impregnated flooring is extremely scuff resistant and dent resistant, and even with sanding it retains a uniform color throughout its lifetime. Maintenance is an occasional buffing or treatment with a special conditioner that revives the finish.

Until recently, prefinished flooring was waxed or coated with polyurethane. This flooring was easy to factory finish but hard for the home owner to maintain. Lately manufacturers have been offering products coated with the more durable urethanes or Swedish finishes. I wouldn't say you shouldn't use wax as a floor finish. A properly maintained waxed floor will outlast any other finish and, in my opinion, it looks better, too. However, even minor wet spills turn a waxed floor into an ice rink so I'd think twice about a waxed floor in the kitchen or bathroom.

When prefinished flooring was first introduced, manufacturers hadn't figured out how to deal with "overwood," the minute differences in thicknesses between one board and next that are evened out when an unfinished floor is sanded (Figure 4). Their solution, if you could call it that, was to chamfer or round over the edges of each board to disguise the thickness variation. The result was dark shadow lines and dirt-catching grooves in the floor. Modern prefinished flooring is made more accurately, so overwood is less of a problem, but a prefinished floor will rarely be as tight as a sanded-in-place floor.

Some manufacturers of prefinished plank with Swedish finish recommend filling the cracks between boards with an oil-based putty. A very light sanding with a buffer and screenback (see Chapter 6 for more on this) smooths the putty, and an additional on-site application of Swedish finish completes the job. Of course, this method defeats the advantage of prefinished flooring, which is to avoid sanding and finishing entirely.

Prefinished flooring is best for living rooms, dining rooms, bedrooms—in general, the low-traffic areas of the house. It's not a good idea for high-traffic areas exposed to water. Some manufacturers even print warning labels on their cartons suggesting that they not be used in such areas. Site-finished flooring, on the other hand, works well in almost any room and will stand up to water.

One other type of flooring worth mentioning is the laminated flooring popular in Europe, where solid-wood flooring is hard to get and expensive. Laminated flooring is really a kind of plywood. It consists of a high-quality veneer glued to a stable substrate, usually plywood or particleboard. Most laminated flooring consists of three plies. It's usually prefinished and is available in strip, plank and parquet. It can be nailed or glued to the subfloor.

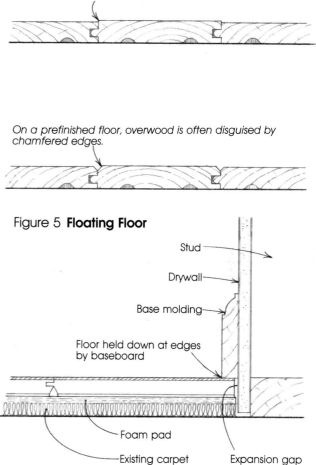

Figure 4 Overwood

On a site-finished floor, overwood caused by thickness variations can be sanded flush.

On a prefinished floor, overwood is often disguised by chamfered edges.

Figure 5 Floating Floor

Stud

Drywall

Base molding

Floor held down at edges by baseboard

Foam pad

Existing carpet

Expansion gap

Several types of laminated flooring are designed to "float" over carpet or soft subfloor, without gluing or nailing. The flooring is held down at the corners by the baseboard. These so-called floating floors, shown in Figure 5, are popular in apartments with concrete floors, where conventional fastening isn't practical.

Because it's less susceptible to changes in moisture, laminated flooring is a good choice below grade or where you expect high moisture conditions. However, it's less resistant than solid wood to major flooding. Sometimes, a floating laminated floor is a last resort in instances where the subfloor isn't suitable for any other kind or floor and where it's just not possible to put down underlayment. The down side of laminated flooring is that it won't withstand the punishment that a solid floor will. The top veneer, while thicker than that used in most plywoods, is still relatively thin. It won't stand up to anything but minimal sanding, so when it's worn out, it has to be replaced.

Water and Wood: a Troublesome Pair

It's amusing to read the advertising hype for furniture polishes. Some insist that wood is a "living" material that needs to "breathe" or be "nourished" by whatever concoction the ad happens to be pushing. The fact is, once it's felled and sawn, a tree and the wood in it are forever dead. That's not to say wood is static; it's just no longer alive.

Much as the human body has veins and arteries to deliver nutrients to its cells, so too does the living tree have a cell structure through which nutrients flow to its various parts. In the living tree, these cells are saturated with sap, which is mostly water with some dissolved minerals from the soil. After the wood is sawn and air or kiln dried, the sap evaporates, leaving the cells and their walls slightly shrunken but

dry and porous. Because the cell walls will reabsorb water and expand in moist conditions, wood is said to be hygroscopic—it responds to changes in atmospheric moisture.

If not accounted for, wood's hygroscopic nature may cause a lot of grief, particularly if dry wood is exposed to liquid water. As illustrated in Figure 6, as wood cells absorb and lose moisture, a board swells and shrinks more across the grain than it does parallel to the grain. This means that with seasonal variations in moisture, a plainsawn board will change far more in width than it will in length or thickness. In contrast, a quartersawn board swells and shrinks more in thickness than in width. Therefore quartersawn stock is considered more moisture stable.

The chart on the facing page shows how the width of a piece of 2¼-in. oak flooring is affected by changes in its moisture content. Here, I should explain what's meant by moisture content in wood. As I explained earlier, wood constantly absorbs and desorbs moisture from the air. However, when a dried board is not giving off or absorbing moisture from the air, it's said to be at equilibrium moisture content (EMC). EMC is expressed as a percentage of the wood's dry weight, so an EMC of 5% really means that 5% of the board's weight is water.

EMC is related to relative humidity (RH). Wood technologists have graphs that precisely tie the two together, but as a rule of thumb, a relative humidity of 25% gives an EMC of 5%, and a

A good soaking from a broken pipe caused more than a foot of cross-grain swelling on the gym floor at left. Restrained by the walls, it buckled and had to be replaced. Potentially troublesome moisture variations between the flooring and the subfloor can be detected by a moisture meter like the one shown below.

Moisture-Induced Movement in 2¼-in. Plainsawn Oak Strip Flooring	
EMC difference	Approximate width change
1%	1/128 in.
3%	1/64 in.
5%	1/32 in.
10%	1/16 in.
14%	3/32 in.
20%	9/64 in.

Figure 6 Moisture-Induced Shrinkage and Swelling

Plainsawn flooring

Tangential growth rings

As wood absorbs and releases water, movement is greatest across the grain.

Quartersawn flooring

Radial growth rings

Quartersawn stock is more moisture stable because it changes more in thickness, less in width.

relative humidity of 75% gives an EMC of 14%. A 50% swing in relative humididity produces an EMC gradient of 10%. This, in turn, translates to a width variation of 1/16 in., as shown in the chart. Not much in a single board but in a floor, all of the boards expand and contract, pushing against each other. Over the width of a 10-ft. wide floor, that amounts to more than 3 in. of total expansion or contraction.

In most houses, at least ones that are heated in the winter and cooled in the summer, the relative-humidity swing will be less than 50%. You will have to allow for expansion and contraction, but most of the time no moisture-related damage will occur. When it does, the results can be spectacular. Flooding caused by broken pipes or seepage through walls is the worst. I've seen swollen floors buckle like hot pavement (see the photo at left on the facing page). In extreme cases, the swelling will actually push the walls out. The opposite extreme is wood heat, which is so dry that it tends to shrink the flooring, opening up cracks.

There are several ways to avoid moisture damage. First, buy dry flooring. Purchase a moisture meter or borrow one from your supplier (most have them) and make sure your flooring is between 6% and 9% moisture content. A $100 moisture meter is cheap insurance against the potential disaster of not recognizing and correcting moisture problems. Don't allow flooring to get rained on. You'd be surprised what even a light rain will do to flooring.

Test the moisture content of the subfloor, too, including concrete floors. The difference between subfloor and flooring shouldn't be greater than 4%. Don't bring flooring into the house until the drywall is well cured. Allow your material to acclimate uncovered in the house for three to six weeks. This should give it plenty of time to reach EMC. Finally, leave an expansion gap between the flooring and the wall, as shown in Figure 5 on p. 25: 1/16 in. of expansion gap for every cross-grain running foot of flooring. The gap will be hidden by the baseboard. Very wide floors will need more of a gap than the baseboard can cover. In this case, undercut the baseboard and/or add a wider shoe molding.

JOB ESTIMATE FORM   JOB # _____   02010

Billing: *Bill Smith*
Good Time Builders
Address: *1311 San Pedro Blvd*
City/St/Zip: *Fed Way WA 98118*
Phone: (H) _____ (W) *328-5700*
Recomended by: Y FL W FHB F/R (PW) NP Other: _____
Date of Bid: *9/6/89* By: *DB*
Date Booked: *10/19/89* Start: *11/29/89*

Job Name: *John & Mary Doe*
Address: *1155 Elm St.*
City/St/Zip: *Seattle, WA. 98008*
Phone: (H) *365-2987* (W) *455-9373*
Map Location: County *Kg* Page *13*
Section *D* Quad *7*
Major Cross Streets: *Elm & Blanchard   (Q. Ann Dist.)*

****

Existing underlayment: *2 layers lino* Over *5/8" Particle* Over *2×6 Car decking*
Existing wood grade: *#1 Com* Color: *Red* Type: *Oak* Size *3/4 × 2 1/4*

	Room	Size			
Existing Hw	*LR*	Size (*18*) X (*12*) =	*216*		
"	"	Size (*4*) X (*6*) =	*24*		*360# Refin*
"	*DR*	Size (*10*) X (*12*) =	*120*		
New Lino over Particle	*KIT*	Size (*8*) X (*12*) =	*96*		
	Nook	Size (*4*) X (*8*) =	*32*		
	"	Size (*3*) X (*12*) =	*36*		*261# New*
	Hall	Size (*3 1/2*) X (*19 1/2*) =	*68*		
	Closet	Size (*2 1/2*) X (*4 1/2*) =	*11*		
	Pantry	Size (*3*) X (*6*) =	*19*		
		Size ( ) X ( ) =			
	Repair (lace into	Size ( ) X ( ) =			
	Existing - Hardway)	Size (*3 1/2*) X (*8*) =	*28 # Repair*		
	DR to Kit	Size ( ) X ( ) =	*Total Sand/Fin 621#*		

Wood-flooring species

Most people have seen so many oak floors that they've come to expect oak to be the only species available for flooring. Oak does account for most of the flooring sold in the United States. Other species, namely maple, pecan, birch, beech, various pines and fir are available, although it may take extra effort to locate sources for these species. More exotic species, like domestic cherry or walnut, mahoganies and other tropical woods, can also be custom manufactured or bought from specialty suppliers.

How to choose a species? It's purely a subjective matter that concerns your own tastes in color and grain. In some locations, say a heavily trafficked hall, some softwoods (pine or fir) may not last, so you may want to use a hardwood like oak or maple. For the same reason, gyms and courts are almost always made of maple. High-moisture areas, basements or below-grade slabs, will do better with species that are moisture stable or with laminated or parquet flooring. In most cases, however, color and grain requirements will govern the selection of species.

The chart on pp. 35-39 shows typical species used for flooring and gives a description of each wood's characteristics. I'd recommend starting with color. If you like warm wood tones and flamboyant grain, red or white oak is a good choice. As you can see in the chart, the grade has everything to do with grain pattern. Reddish hues dominate red oak flooring, while white oak is lighter with a tan to light brown color. However, expect considerable variation within a given lot of either red or white oak, and don't be surprised to find an occasional white oak board in a bundle or red oak flooring, or vice versa.

White oak is slightly less moisture stable than red oak, which means it will expand and contract more during seasonal moisture changes. For this reason, a white oak floor might be "noisier" than a red oak floor, snapping and popping a bit until the boards reach equilibrium moisture content. Red oak is more porous and slightly softer than white oak. Because of this, red oak absorbs more stain than does white oak, producing a very noticeable contrast between boards in the same floor. Also, red oak will consume a lot more stain and finish than white oak.

220 Power Source: BASEMENT LAUNDRY ROOM

DETAIL WORK: SCRAPE (DON'T EDGER AROUND TILE WORK IN ENTRY NEXT TO LR. BAG OFF FROM DUST ON T&M BASIS

Job Rating: 5 6 7 8 9 10
Client Rating: 5 6 7 8 9 10

Materials: (1) 4' NOSING HALL TO BASEMENT
(1) 3/4" REDUCER @ POWDER ROOM DOOR

Special Instructions and Equipment Needed: TAKE EDGER DURING INSTALL REPAIR TO DETERMINE BEST COLOR MATCH TO EXISTING, TOE KICK EDGER FOR KIT & RAISED HEARTH IN LR

****

JOB COSTING

OPTION 1: LACE INTO EXISTING HW IN DR W/NEW FLOOR IN KIT. INSTALL NEW #1 COM RED OAK IN KIT/NOOK/PANTRY/HALL. SAND STAIN W/OWNER SELECTED NON PIGMENTED COLOR REFINISH LR/DR/KIT/NOOK/PANTRY AND HALL W/2 CTS SWEDISH FINISH

$ 1,000,00 (plus tax)

OPTION 2: SAME AS OPTION #1 EXCEPT W/3 CTS FINISH

$ 1,500,00 (plus tax)

Red oak's stain-absorption properties can be a plus with heavy pigmented stains, such as whites or greys. These stains consist of large particles that don't penetrate deeply into the wood's large pores. When a wide color variation is wanted or a pigmented heavy stain is being used, red oak will probably produce better results. White oak is more evenly colored to begin with, and it accepts stains more evenly, if sparingly. White oak isn't as good a choice as red when a wide color variation is desired, but the final result will be more uniform.

Hard maples are also widely available for flooring, mostly for gyms and sports floors but in residential applications, too. The light color and subtle grain pattern are a nice change of pace from oak. Two varieties of maple are available, one grown throughout the South and lower Midwest and the other in the upper Midwest. Both are similar in appearance—creamy white in color with tight, relatively subdued grain—but the northern variety is denser and harder. As the chart on pp. 35-39 shows, maple is one of the hardest species used for flooring. Like white oak, it's not very porous but accepts most finishes evenly. Because maple has low rot and moisture resistance, it's a poor choice for wet areas like bathrooms or below-grade applications.

Three other hardwood species listed in the chart that might turn up with a diligent search of suppliers are pecan, beech and birch. These three are similar to maple, in that they're very hard and have dense, subdued grain. Depending on your tastes in color, any of the three would be a good alternative to the rather pronounced grain of red oak and white oak. Also included in the chart are the most popular softwoods: fir and the pines.

Estimating

Calculating the amount of flooring you need for a job isn't particularly difficult. All it takes is careful measuring and some way to record your calculations. Because I have to estimate complex jobs, some with many rooms, I devised the job-estimate form shown here. A scratch pad will do just as well, especially for a small job.

To estimate accurately, first determine the net square footage of the area to be covered. In a square room, this is simple. Just multiply the room's width by its length. Oddly shaped or angular rooms can be divided into smaller squares (Figure 7). For the rare circular or triangular room, square off the angles or, if you're really obsessive about accuracy, use the formulas for calculating the area of a circle or triangle. In the kitchen or bathroom, the ends of the flooring can "run wild" or untrimmed beneath the cabinets to within a foot of the wall; or, if the cabinets are already installed, the ends can simply butt to the toe plates. Allow for one of these methods in your square-footage measurements.

To calculate the square footage of strip or plank flooring required, add about 5% or 6% to the net coverage area. Add 10% if you're using parquet. This allows 2% to 3% for cutting waste and another 2% to 3% for culls. If you want to "grade up" a little by picking the very best pieces in the bundles, add 10% to net coverage. A floor that will be laid on the diagonal or one that's "cut up" with lots of angles or cabinets and walls should have about 15% to 25% extra added to the net coverage. Similarly, add 15% to 20% to specially ordered or custom-made flooring so you won't run the risk of falling a few boards short only to find that your flooring is out of stock or no longer made. Plan to stash the leftovers in the attic, for repairs.

As I mentioned above, unfinished flooring comes in bundles four boards deep and three wide. To convert a bundle's contents to square footage, first figure "bundle feet." Bundle lengths are figured by averaging the random lengths of each piece. Because the rules allow pieces 6 in. over or 6 in. under the nominal length, a 2-ft. bundle might have some 18-in. pieces and some 30-in. pieces. I have developed a rule of thumb for quickly calculating the square footage that a bundle of strip flooring will cover: just multiply its nominal length by 2.25. A 6-ft. bundle, then, will cover 13.5 sq. ft. You would therefore need 233 bundle feet to cover a 500-sq. ft. floor (figuring 5% for waste and culls). For parquet floors, the area coverage is often printed on the cartons. If it isn't, multiply the area of each tile by the number of tiles in each box.

When you've decided how much flooring to buy, the next question is where to buy it. A couple of hours spent on the phone will pay off. Make a quick scratch-pad chart listing species, grade, bundles sizes and price. Call the full-service lumberyards and discount home centers first. Expect to find wide swings in price and availability of flooring types and grades. Where demand is strong, the local home center may carry lots of flooring at competitive prices. With any luck, they'll have a salesperson who knows flooring nomenclature.

Call the flooring contractors in your area, too. These days, many are happy to sell retail at very favorable prices. I find that I'm frequently willing to give a customer a good deal on surplus stock that's just taking up space in my warehouse. Don't shy away from dealing with a contractor on such necessities as nailer and sander rental, adhesives and finishing supplies. A contractor is more likely to have a good selection of these items than the local rental store.

Tools

To install flooring, you can get by with a good basic carpenter's toolkit plus the floor-sanding equipment that I'll describe in Chapter 6. With the basic kit, you'll have to drive and set nails by hand—certainly doable but no picnic. Better to have power nailers for both face and blind nailing. You can rent these, either from the flooring supplier or a rental shop.

The basic kit starts with measuring and marking tools. You should have at least a 20-ft. tape measure, a long straightedge, framing and try squares, a bevel gauge for setting off angles and a chalkbox for marking layout lines. Whether you drive nails by hand or with a power nailer, you'll be doing a lot of hammering, so a I recommend springing for a good-quality hammer. I like a 20-oz.

Figure 7 **Measuring and Estimating**

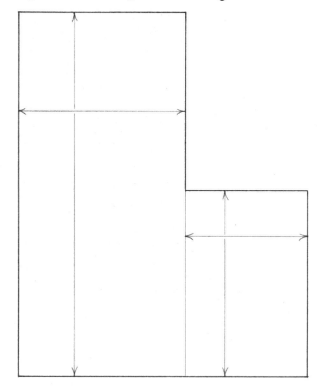

To calculate the area of odd-shaped floor plans, measure them as separate squares or rectangles. Add 5% to 6% to net area to allow for waste.

The floor mechanic's basic toolkit, shown above, consists of measuring and marking tools (left), and a hammer, nailsets and a large screwdriver for prying strips into place (center). Power tools include a drill, a chopsaw, a sabre saw, a small circular saw and a router. Knee pads, safety glasses and hearing protectors are essential safety equipment. For fastening borders, headers and plank flooring, the author uses combination bits, shown below, that simultaneously bore a pilot hole and counterbore for wooden plugs.

smooth-face hammer. Along with the hammer, have nail sets in all three sizes. Make sure the set's cupped heads are in good shape and not cracked or spalled. Other assorted hand tools you'll need include a utility knife, at least one large screwdriver for prying and a stapler. A couple of planes, a block and a jack, are handy for trimming flooring. Chisels in several sizes will be useful for chopping underlayment or notching flooring around obstacles. Basic equipment is shown in the photo above.

Fur cutting flooring to length, a finish carpenter's chopsaw is hard to beat, although a circular saw, sabre saw or even a table saw will do the job, too. A chopsaw can be set up on the floor nearby and worked from the kneeling position. With a table saw, you'll have stand up to make each cut. After a hundred cuts, you'll feel it. The table saw is excellent, however, for ripping flooring to width, and sabre saw will also rip. A router (½ hp minimum) with an assortment of bits is a good idea, too, particularly for doing inlay work.

Headers and borders are often screwed and plugged, so you'll need a set of bits and counterbores to bore the holes, plus a plug cutter if you want to make your own plugs. The W. L. Fuller Company makes combination bit and counterbore sets (for their address, see the Resource Guide on p. 132). Buy at least two of the size so if one breaks, you won't get stuck. Unless you have combination bits, it's a good idea to have two electric drills, one for the bit and one for the counterbore.

Specialty tools I'd recommend having are two power nailers (a face nailer and a side nailer), a pneumatic nailer (optional), a jamb saw (power or hand) and a powder-

Although not absolutely necessary, flooring will go faster with some of the specialty tools shown at left, including power nailers (top) and hand and power jamb saws (bottom). For blind nailing, the power nailer's angled baseplate, shown below, fits over the top of each strip's tongue. A sharp blow drives and sets the nail.

The jamb saw's arbor nut is nearly flush with the blade, allowing it to cut very near the floor.

actuated fastening system if you'll be installing a floor over concrete. The power nailers are mechanically assisted nailers with a plunger that drives and sets the nail with a single hammer blow. One type has an angled head that nestles next to the flooring's tongue for blind nailing; the other sits flat on the board for face nailing.

Both types of power nailers dispense barbed fasteners through a magazine that fits into the back of the nailer. On a very large job with a lot of face nailing, I like to have a pneumatic nailer capable of driving finish nails. This is an excellent tool for tacking underlayment, face nailing flooring and installing trim. Like the power nailers, it can be rented, along with the compressor that runs it.

As shown in the photo above, the jamb saw looks sort of like a router. Instead of a bit, it has a horizontally mounted circular saw whose height can be adjusted to saw off baseboards and door casings so that flooring can be slipped underneath. A jamb saw is a real worksaver in remodel work, since the alternative is to remove all of the trim, then reinstall it after the flooring is done.

Safety

As the building trades go, flooring is no more dangerous than frame carpentry, trim work or plumbing. It's just that in flooring, you're likely to get hurt in different ways.

Believe it or not, some of the nastiest injuries in flooring work come from handling the material. Kiln-dried oak is brittle and prone to splintering. If you're not careful, you can pick up terribly painful slivers of wood. Always wear gloves when loading or moving bundles of flooring. And try to get some help when unloading to avoid muscle strains. Those bundles are heavier than they look.

Because there's so much hammering going on, a careless moment can cost you a bashed finger between the power nailer's plunger head and the hammer. This is a common injury. Keep your hands well clear when driving nails. Also, don't use a steel hammer to whack the power nailer. It's liable to dislodge steel chips that can cause an eye or skin injury. I always wear safety glasses when nailing or sawing, just in case.

Without a doubt, the most dangerous tool is the chopsaw. It's a powerful tool whose blade can cut off a finger in an instant. Keep your hands well clear when the blade is turning, and don't remove or disable the guard. It's there to protect you, and of all the power-tool guards, the chopsaw guard is probably the most effective. The chopsaw is designed for crosscutting, either at 90° or at angles. Don't try to rip with it. It just won't work.

Sanding equipment deserves special mention. Floor sanders are incredibly powerful. Although it won't cut off a finger, a runaway floor sander can do fearsome damage, knocking holes in walls and generally flattening anything that gets in its way. To keep out of harm's way (and the sander's way), always leave the machine unplugged until the moment you use it. This is especially important when your fingers are near the drum while changing belts. In the videotape (and in Chapter 6) I go into more detail about sander safety. Make sure you understand the important points before proceeding.

At the finishing stage, dust, fumes and odor will be a problem. During sanding, I wear a nuisance-dust mask. This is nothing but a paper filter that prevents most of the particles from reaching the lungs. It's not a chemical filter. For that kind of protection, you need an organic-vapor respirator with clean filters. I always wear a respirator when brushing on any kind of finish, regardless of how benign the manufacturer claims the material to be. It's not a good idea to use the organic respirator as a dust mask, however. The dust will clog the filters and make them less effective as chemical barriers.

Domestic Species Used for Flooring

Species	Ash, white	Beech, American	Birch, yellow
Habitat	Central to eastern U. S.	Central to eastern U. S. and southern Canada.	Southeastern to south-central Canada and northeastern to north-central U. S.
Characteristics	Heartwood is dark brown to brown. Sapwood is white to brownish white. Similar in appearance to white oak, but frequently more yellow. Straight and fairly open grained with occasional wavy figure. Strong contrast between growth rings in plainsawn boards.	Heartwood is mostly reddish brown. Sapwood is generally pale white. Mostly straight-grained and close-grained wood with a fine, even texture. American beech is somewhat coarser than its European counterpart.	Heartwood is light brown to tan tinged with reddish tones, particularly in latewood. Sapwood is creamy yellow to pale white. Colors vary considerably among boards. Straight, close grain with a fine even texture, with occasional curly grain or wavy figure in some boards.
Durability	Ash is elastic, tough and has excellent shock resistance. It's fairly moisture stable.	Beech is elastic and has a strong shock resistance but is very susceptible to moisture-induced movement.	Strong, dense and hard. Excellent for flooring, but poor moisture stability.
Cost and availability	Not a traditional flooring material, ash has not been generally available until recently. Specialty wood-flooring dealers and some lumberyards regularly carry unfinished strip. Moderately priced.	Although once readily available as flooring, beech is now a special-order item in unfinished strip only. Moderately priced.	Available in unfinished strip or parquet, mostly as a special-order or custom-milled material. Moderate to expensive.

Species	Cherry, American black	Fir, Douglas	Hemlock, western
Habitat	Southeastern Canada and northern and central U. S.	Western U. S. and western Canada. Most Douglas fir used for flooring grows in the northwestern U. S. and southwestern Canada.	Western U. S. and western Canada.
Characteristics	Heartwood is pinkish brown to dark reddish brown. Sapwood is light brown to pale white with a light pinkish tone. Normally a straight-grained material with a fine and even texture, boards are frequently figured with wavy grain.	Heartwood is yellowish tan to light brown. Sapwood is tan to white. Some boards develop a slight pinkish to bright salmon color when finished with some products. Nearly all fir flooring is vertical-grain or riftsawn clear-grade material. Grain is normally straight, with an occasional wavy or spiral texture.	Heartwood is tan to light brown with darker reddish-colored latewood bands. Sapwood is pale to nearly white, with occasional greyish streaks. Like Douglas fir, western hemlock sometimes develops a bright salmon color when finished. Hemlock is straight grained with a fine, even texture.
Durability	Fairly durable and stable in use but somewhat softer than oak.	Durable but easily dented. Fairly moisture stable, compared to oak. Boards are somewhat brittle and splinter quite easily, particularly with age.	Somewhat durable as light-duty flooring, but softer and weaker than Douglas fir. Fairly stable.
Cost and availability	A special order in unfinished strip, plank or parquet. Expensive.	Commonly available in the western U. S. and Canada at most lumber retailers or wood-flooring specialty dealers in several sizes as unfinished strip or plank. Also available in end-grain block flooring. Moderately priced.	Commonly available in the western U. S. and Canada at lumber retailers and wood-flooring dealers in various widths and thicknesses in unfinished plank. Also available in end-grain block flooring. Inexpensive.

Hickory	Koa	Maple, hard (sugar)	Maple, soft
Southeastern Canada and northeastern U. S. to southwestern Mexico.	Hawaiian Islands.	Southern Canada and north-central to northeastern U. S.	Most of U. S. and Canada.
Heartwood is brown to reddish brown with occasional black streaks. Sapwood is white to creamy white with pinkish tones. The higher grades of hickory are cut from the light-colored sapwood, where only minor pinkish-toned late growth distracts from the smooth grain tone. Hickory is a tight-grained and somewhat rough-textured wood with a modest grain definition.	Very similar to walnut in grain, texture and appearance, though not as hard. Grain is frequently figured with curly, burl or fiddleback. Trees are subject to silicon impregnation from windswept ridges, creating unique figures in boards. Finished boards frequently have a glowing, radiant appearance.	Heartwood is creamy white to reddish brown. Some boards may have occasional streaks of dark brown or black. Sapwood is pale to creamy white. Occasionally maple shows quilted, fiddleback, curly or bird's-eye figure, but grain is generally subdued. Generally, the lighter the color, the higher the grade.	Heartwood varies by variety from light tan to brown with reddish patches or streaks. Sapwood is pale to creamy white. Soft maple normally shows more black streaking than hard maple, and is straight grained with not nearly as much figure variation as hard maple; finishes to lower luster.
Extremely durable and resilient. Pound for pound, one of the toughest woods around.	Durable and generally stable under average changes in moisture.	Extremely hard and resistant to abrasion; excellent for sports floors. Medium movement with average changes in moisture.	Not as abrasion resistant as hard maple but provides a durable indoor floor for most purposes. Good moisture stability.
Not commonly available outside of specialty wood-flooring dealers. A special order in unfinished strip flooring for most shops. Not normally available in parquet or plank except in custom milling. Moderately expensive.	Special-order item or through custom milling from specialty wood-flooring dealers in strip, parquet and plank. More readily available in Hawaiian Islands in both unfinished strip, plank and parquet. Very expensive.	Commonly available in most commodity types and sizes of flooring including parquet. Available by special order in fancy parquet, plank and some veneers. Moderately priced.	Not normally stocked, but soft maples are often used as a less expensive alternative to hard maple. Moderately priced.

Species	Oak, red	Oak, white	Pecan
Habitat	South-central to eastern Canada and most of the U. S.	Southern Canada and most of the U. S. Most white oak used for flooring is grown in south-central Canada or mid-southern to southeastern U. S.	Southeastern U. S. and Mexico.
Characteristics	Heartwood is dark brown to pink. Most pieces have a somewhat reddish tone. Sapwood is pale tan to white. There is considerable variation among boards in color and grain texture. Plainsawn boards have a plumed or flare grain appearance. Quartersawing produces a characteristic crossgrain "fleck" sometimes called tiger ray or butterflies.	Heartwood is light brown to tan. Some boards may have a pinkish tint, others a slight greyish cast. Sapwood is white to reddish yellow. There is considerable variation among boards in color and grain texture but less than with red oak. White oak absorbs finishing materials more evenly than red oak but is slightly less moisture stable.	Heartwood is dark to reddish brown with occasional darker streaks. The sapwood is usually creamy white and graded higher than the darker heartwood. Mostly tight grained and rough textured, but has occasional wavy or irregular nature. Pecan is frequently mixed with hickory by many flooring mills.
Durability	Quite durable compared to most softwoods. Less durable than white oak. Somewhat moisture unstable, but more moisture stable than white oak.	Quite durable compared to most softwoods, and more durable than red oak.	Hard and strong with good moisture stability.
Cost and availability	Commonly available in nearly all types, styles and sizes of flooring including parquet, strip, plank and veneer in both unfinished and prefinished varieties. Moderately priced.	Commonly available in nearly all types, styles and sizes of flooring including parquet, strip, plank and veneer in both unfinished and prefinished varieties. Moderately priced.	Strip flooring is generally available from specialty wood-flooring dealers. Parquet and plank not commonly available. Expensive.

Pine, eastern white	Pine, ponderosa	Pine, southern yellow	Walnut, American black
Eastern U. S. and southeastern Canada.	Western U. S. and western Canada.	Southeastern to south-central U. S.	Southern Canada and most of U. S. Most walnut used for flooring grows in central to south-central U. S.
A soft, even-textured wood with a straight grain and indeterminate growth rings. Heartwood ranges from light and pale yellow to reddish brown. Resin ducts appear as fine dark brown lines.	Heartwood varies from reddish brown to a strong yellow with resin ducts appearing as fine dark brown lines. Sapwood ranges from a pale soft yellow to a light yellow. Some boards may have a bird's-eye figure similar to maple. Frequently used as knotty pine for interior woodwork.	The four major varieties of pitch pine or southern yellow pine have many of the same characteristics as Douglas fir. Heartwood varies from light yellow/orange to reddish brown or yellowish brown in longleaf or loblolly pine. Sapwood is light tan to yellowish white. Old-growth lumber in these varieties yields substantially higher density and more stable flooring than second-growth material.	Heartwood ranges from a deep rich dark brown to a purplish black. Sapwood is much lighter tan to light brown. Most mills steam walnut prior to kiln drying to produce a more even color. Mostly straight grained, but some boards can have figure such as burl or curly grain. There is considerable variation in color among boards, especially in lower grades and from material that has not been steamed.
Easily dented and not very durable even as light-duty flooring, but good moisture stability.	Durable, light-duty flooring, but dents easily. Moderate moisture stability.	Fairly durable, though not as resistant to scuffs, dents and abrasions as the hardwoods.	Durable but not as dent resistant as oak. Exceptionally stable, with very little movement from average changes in moisture.
Although a common flooring material in very inexpensive homes of the last century, eastern white pine is now rarely stocked. It's readily obtainable as inexpensive shelving material that can be tongued and grooved into planking or left square edged, then face nailed or screwed and plugged into place. Inexpensive.	Not routinely stocked as flooring but can be custom milled without undue expense. Moderately priced.	Available as unfinished strip and plank flooring in a variety of widths and thicknesses through specialty wood-flooring dealers and some lumberyards as special orders. Moderately priced.	Normally available in unfinished parquet, strip and in various plank widths as a special order from wood-flooring specialty shops. Also available in fancy parquet patterns as a special order or custom mill. Very expensive.

The subfloor must be flat and defect-free before flooring is laid. A drum sander fitted with a coarse belt flattens irregularities in the car decking.

Preparation and Underlayment

Chapter 3

Around the Seattle area, I've gotten a reputation as a floor-repair specialist, probably because I've been willing (or foolish enough) to take on fix-up jobs that other contractors won't even bid. People who have hardwood floors know that replacing them is a major investment. Most will go to great lengths to salvage a damaged floor. It's challenging work.

The worst cases are water-damaged floors, where a good soaking has swollen and buckled the boards. Not an easy save, but possible. There is a lot of minor repair work, too, such as quieting squeaks or replacing damaged boards or parquet tiles. Sanding and refinishing are the bread-and-butter elements of restoration work that often follow other fixes. Although I didn't intend it that way, doing repair work has taught me a lot about how not to install a wood floor. Time after time, premature damage or degrade is caused by poor preparation or an inadequate understanding of wood-floor mechanics. It's amazing how a minor oversight, such as poor ventilation in a foundation crawl space, will later manifest itself in a vexing (and expensive) floor problem.

Many floor problems are avoidable by picking the right floor for the application and installing it over a correctly prepared subfloor. If there's such a thing as a floorman's axiom, it's this: A hardwood floor is no better than what's under it. And what's under it will probably be one of three major kinds of subfloors: concrete slab, wooden plank or plywood decking. Types of plywood include particleboard and oriented strand board, or OSB. Each type will require its own kind of preparation, depending on the flooring material you want to use. In some cases, the subfloor you happen to have won't accommodate the flooring you want, so you'll have to pick another kind of flooring or install suitable underlayment. Always ask your supplier about subfloor/finish-floor compatibility.

Removing the old floor

Whatever the subfloor, it needs to be flat, level and dry. It also needs to be strong enough to support the weight of the finish flooring without sagging and sound enough to accept whatever fasteners you plan to use. Some subfloors, such as the plywood decking in a new house, shouldn't need much work, other than whacking down a protruding nail here and there. Remodel work, on the other hand, can be the stuff of nightmares, particularly if an existing finished floor hides some unpleasant surprises in the subfloor. Old cold-air returns, abandoned heating registers or holes from old radiators are just a few of the problems remodelers may face.

The floor I picked as a sample for the video that accompanies this book is a typical remodel job. The kitchen and dining room were covered with sheet vinyl over particleboard nailed to the subfloor. The living room and hall had the same ⅜-in. particleboard underlayment, but topped with carpet. The subfloor is 1½-in. tongue-and-groove Douglas fir planking, called car decking on the West Coast.

Before I could even get a look at the car decking, however, the old floor had to be stripped away. I could have nailed my new flooring on top of the sheet vinyl. Since the particleboard underlayment was only ⅜ in. thick, the nails would have penetrated into the car decking. I didn't do this for several reasons. First, I wanted a uniform height between my new floor and existing flooring in adjoining rooms, and I didn't want to reduce the height of the toe space under my cabinet toe kicks. Second, I don't like depending on the holding strength of flooring fasteners through ⅜-in. particleboard. Finally, the cushion effect of hardwood over sheet vinyl causes excessive deflection between boards, which would be a real problem with the Swedish finish I planned to use.

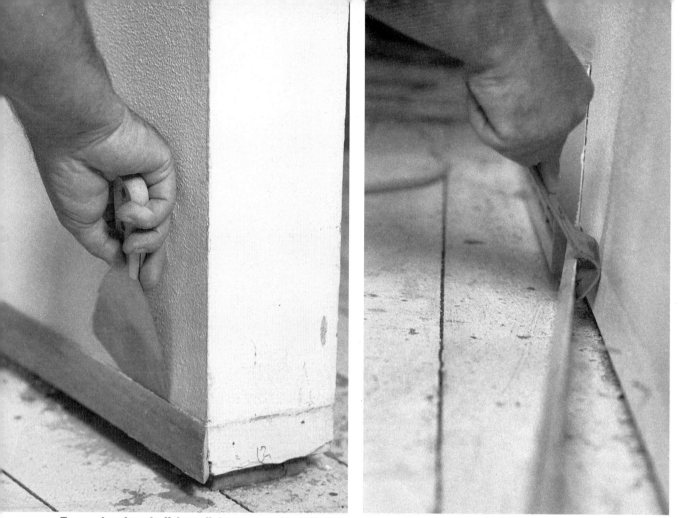

To ease baseboard off the wall, insert a spackle knife between the molding and the wall (left). A prybar completes removal (right). If force is required to pry the baseboard, protect the wall with a scrap block behind the prybar.

To begin, clear the room of furniture and remove the baseboards from the wall, as shown in the photos above. If new baseboards are part of your plans, just pry the old ones off without worrying about breaking them. Replacing the base, however, sometimes means new door casings too. If that sounds like more work than you bargained for, salvage the old base by coaxing it off the wall with a pry-bar. Old baseboard is dry and brittle, so take your time. To keep from marring the wall, hold a scrap block or spackle knife between the wall and the back of your bar. Number each piece so it can be placed back where it belongs later. Always score the paint line along the baseboard wall joint with a utility knife. This will keep an adhered paint film from prying off the drywall's paper facing.

Unless it's glued down, carpet is usually the easiest finish flooring material to remove. Pry up a corner near a tack strip and just pull up the whole thing, pad and all. Most of the time, you'll find the subfloor underneath to be dry but filthy, regardless of how fastidious the house-cleaning has been. If you're really lucky, you'll find an old hardwood floor that someone decided to hide beneath a

carpet rather than refinish. It happens. Otherwise, expect to find plywood, car decking or concrete. Carpet over concrete is often bad news. It may be glued to the slab, which means hours of tedious scraping, either with a steel-blade painter's scraper or a long-handled scraper that you might be able to rent from your flooring dealer. Either way, you have to remove every last bit of the pad.

Sheet vinyl or resilient tile is no picnic to remove, either. I always hope that whoever installed the stuff was lazy and just rolled it out with a few tacks at the corner to hold it down. Too bad that was rarely the case. Usually, sheet vinyl is glued to the subfloor with mastic, whose hardness depends on how old it is. Brittle mastic will yield to a wide chisel—you can chip away at the mastic and take the linoleum with it in small pieces. Newer mastic may be pliable enough to allow the linoleum to be lifted off in larger pieces.

Resilient tile will almost always be glued. It comes up the way it went down: one piece at a time, with a scraper. A word of caution here: Some older resilient floors and adhesives contain asbestos. This is definitely nasty stuff

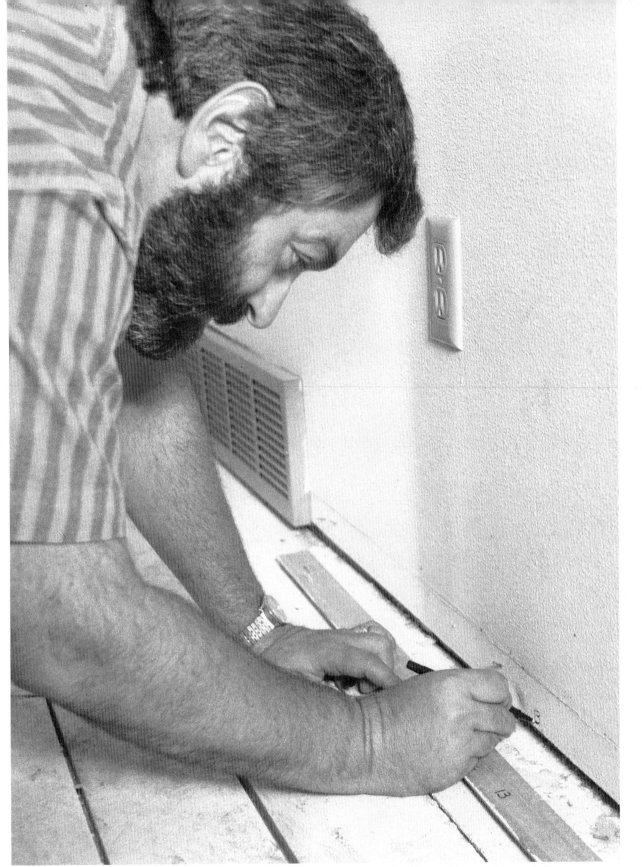

So the baseboard can be reinstalled correctly, label the molding and the wall with matching numbers or letters.

To remove the old floor, saw through the underlayment to the subfloor, then pry up both the underlayment and linoleum at the same time (top left). To avoid removing cabinets, chop a line along the bases with a chisel (above), then pry up the underlayment (left).

that's been implicated in cancer and asbestosis. In some states, before they begin work, contractors are required to get an inspection certifying that asbestos has been safely removed from any dwelling where its presence is suspected. If you have any doubts about the flooring you're about to remove, check the Yellow Pages. This issue has gotten enough attention to have spawned asbestos-testing labs, even in small towns.

I will discuss underlayments later in this chapter (see pp. 50-51), but for for now, suffice it to say that I consider particleboard an unsuitable underlayment for hardwood flooring, except for some types of glue-down parquet. When I discovered it under the linoleum on this job, I didn't bother trying to save it. With a circular saw's cutting depth set to the particleboard's thickness, I sawed the floor into sections and pried them up with a wrecking bar. The kitchen cabinets were installed on top of the finish floor, but rather than remove them, I chopped and chiseled the particleboard flush with the base of each cabinet, as shown in the photos above.

After the baseboard is removed and you've gotten down to clean subfloor, check it thoroughly for loose or deflecting boards. These should be renailed or replaced as needed. Unless new doors and trim are yet to be installed, the next step is to trim the door casings to allow the new flooring to slip beneath. You can remove the casing or take the easy road by trimming them in place with a jamb saw. You may be able to rent an electric or hand jamb saw from your flooring supplier. If not, a fine-toothed handsaw or Japanese dovetail saw will work as well. To determine how much the casing should be trimmed back, use a piece of flooring as a depth gauge. If underlayment is required, you'll have to allow for its thickness too. The photos below show electric and hand jamb saws in use.

On the power jamb saw (left), the width of cut is set to the thickness of the flooring plus the underlayment thickness, if any will be used. Use a scrap piece of of actual flooring as a depth gauge for the hand jamb saw (above). The photo below shows the off-cut casing.

Checking the subfloor

I spend a lot of time looking over a subfloor. Even if it takes as long to repair the subfloor as it does to install the finish flooring, I never cut corners. Next to moisture, defective subfloors are responsible for more floor problems than anything else. Check the subfloor for level and flatness (Figure 8). Ideally, it should be both. Most of the time, flat will be a lot easier to achieve than level. Even in new houses, settling inevitably cants the floor in one plane or another, or perhaps in several planes at once. Check the subfloor at several spots with a 6-ft. level. In the floorman's dream world, the subfloor won't be more than 1/8 in. out of level over a 10-ft. run. In the real world, the runout will be more than that. Maybe a lot more.

What to do about it? Unless the runout is glaringly obvious or the floor is conspicuously twisted, I usually ignore it. What with settling, level is a fleeting thing and relative at that. How can you tell if the floor is slightly out of level without sighting it against something that is? As long as the floor is fairly flat, there's no structural or aesthetic reason for it be perfectly level. Where settling is so severe that shoring of the frame or foundation is necessary, then go ahead and aim for level. In some circumstances, where underlayment is necessary, the subfloor can be shimmed, as shown in Figure 9. While shims do the job, the cure may be worse than the disease. You now have to deal with the height gain created by the shims and match the higher floor to adjacent flooring. Tapered reducers between the two floors are the usual solution.

Out-of-flatness in a subfloor is more troublesome than out-of-level. Strip or plank flooring won't always bridge irregularities, resulting in overwood, looseness, creaking and open joints. Walk the floor carefully and look for dips and rises. A long straightedge, plywood or a 2x4, spotted on the floor at various points, will help locate irregularities. Very gentle dips, say 1/8 in. over a 5-ft. to 10-ft. run, are acceptable. Even minor abrupt changes (1/8 in. or so) between pieces of plywood can result in problems, particularly if flooring is to run parallel with the variation. Sharp changes in plane will need attention. A good rule is that if your shoe catches on it, you should deal with it. On a car-decked subfloor like the one shown here, walk the floor and look for loose planks first, especially where the butt ends meet. Fasten down loose boards with 16d nails or screws.

Figure 8 **Checking the Subfloor**

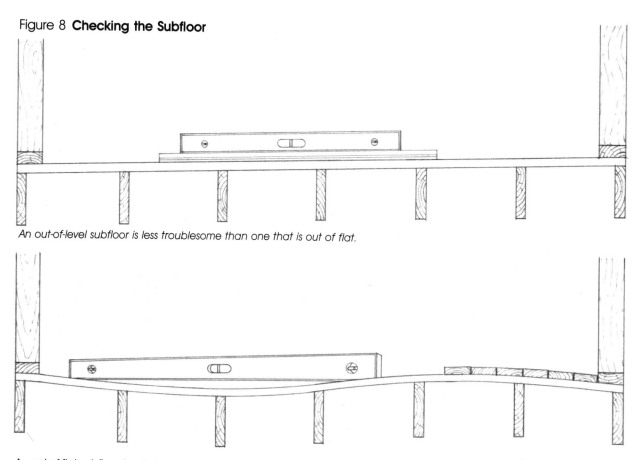

An out-of-level subfloor is less troublesome than one that is out of flat.

An out-of-flat subfloor leads to open joints, loose boards.

Figure 9 **Shimming a Subfloor**

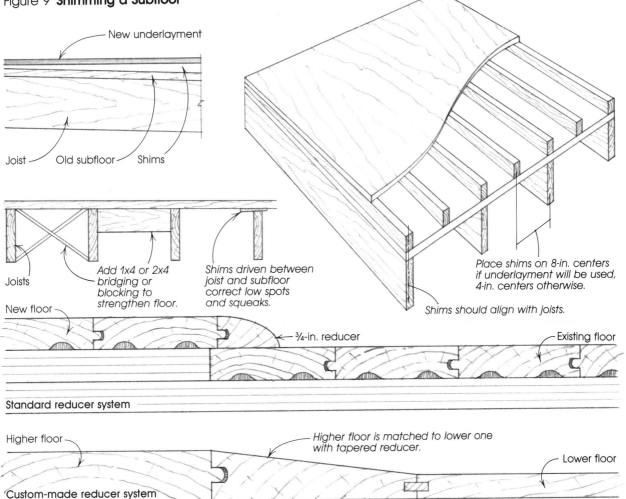

New underlayment

Joist — Old subfloor — Shims

Joists

Add 1x4 or 2x4 bridging or blocking to strengthen floor.

Shims driven between joist and subfloor correct low spots and squeaks.

Place shims on 8-in. centers if underlayment will be used, 4-in. centers otherwise.

Shims should align with joists.

New floor

¾-in. reducer

Existing floor

Standard reducer system

Higher floor

Higher floor is matched to lower one with tapered reducer.

Lower floor

Custom-made reducer system

Make sure that the nails go into joists, or you're wasting your time. Where planks are tight but overwood exists, mark the spot, and then sand it flush with a floor sander. If you find dips that aren't practical to sand or fill, mark them too, then arrange your flooring to bridge the entire dip instead of butting in or near the dip. Plywood decks should be treated just like planking. Walk the floor and nail any loose spots, especially where the plywood sheets meet. It's almost impossible to overnail a subfloor, so if in doubt, nail.

Exterior plywood is normally used for floor decks. It's made with waterproof adhesive but it will still swell unevenly when exposed to rain before the house is closed in, creating overwood between sheets. Excessive weathering will cause delamination, resulting in a spongy subfloor. It's best to replace such sections. As with car decking, sand any plywood overwood flush. With car decking or plywood, creaks and loose spots can also be fixed with thin wedges inserted between the joists and the subfloor

Any looseness in the subfloor should be corrected by nailing or screwing the loose pieces. Make sure the fasteners are driven into joists.

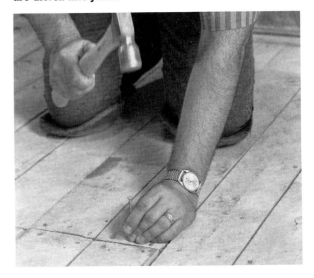

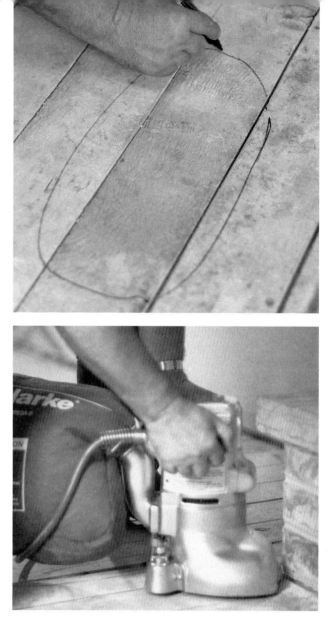

To flatten severe overwood, sand at 45° to the car decking (above). Minor variations can be flattened by sanding with the grain, as shown in the photo on p. 40. Low spots that can't be sanded flat should be marked (above right), and flooring strips or planks should be laid to bridge them. Avoid butting the ends of flooring over a low spot. Level high corners with the edger, as shown at right.

or by bridging between joists. This assumes that you have access to the joists, which might not be the case in a second-floor room. Adding bridging or blocking, as shown in Figure 9 on p. 47, not only reduces creaking and flexing but will also strengthen the subfloor.

Localized high spots or corners can be knocked down with the edger. Concrete subfloors are more difficult to flatten. Small ridges or variations can be corrected with the floor sander fitted with 12-grit to 36-grit paper. Watch out for the dust though. It's talcum-powder fine, and unless you seal off the adjacent rooms, the dust will seep into every nook and cranny. Really wavy floors can be ground flat with a concrete grinder (rent one or hire someone who has one) or filled with commercial leveling compounds. The Resource Guide on p. 134 lists a few sources for these compounds.

Moisture and ventilation. Mechanical defects in subfloors (overwood, twists, flexing and loose boards) are easy to see and fix compared to the wood floor's prime enemy: moisture. As I explained in Chapter 2, the flooring itself should be allowed to acclimate to equilibrium moisture content before it's installed. The subflooring too should be at an equilibrium moisture content, not just recently heated after months of exposure to the elements and wet masonry, tile, drywall and paint.

Wood subfloors are easy to check. Just jab the probes of a moisture meter into the floor at several spots and average the results. If excessively high readings are obtained, check for leaks or spills in the area. During the winter, an overly moist subfloor can be dried out by closing up the house and running the heat for a few weeks. Air conditioning during the summer will do the same

Test a new concrete floor for moisture content by taping a square of clear polyethylene on the slab. If the plastic fogs with condensation overnight, the concrete is too wet for a wood floor.

Figure 10 **Crawl-Space Ventilation**

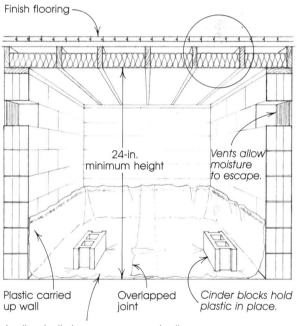

Finish flooring

24-in. minimum height

Vents allow moisture to escape.

Plastic carried up wall

Overlapped joint

Cinder blocks hold plastic in place.

6-mil polyethylene over exposed soil

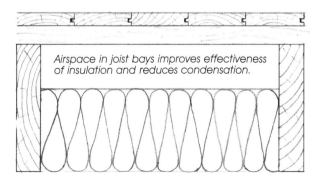

Airspace in joist bays improves effectiveness of insulation and reduces condensation.

thing. If the moisture content between the flooring and subflooring varies more than 6% to 8%, stack the flooring in the house so it can acclimate to the new level. Once the two are within 4% moisture content of each other, it's okay to proceed.

New concrete floors release so much moisture that I don't even consider laying a floor on one for at least 60 days or more. New or old, though, a slab will have to be checked for moisture. Some moisture meters have special probes for concrete testing. Another way is to tape a foot-square piece of clear plastic sheet on the slab. If the plastic fogs with condensation overnight, the slab is too wet. Allow it to cure for another few weeks and try again.

You can gently force-dry a green slab with ventilation and dehumidifiers or heat. I recommend consulting a professional flooring or concrete contractor before attempting to force-dry a slab. You risk cracking the concrete if it's done improperly. Parquet floors are often glued directly to slabs. This is acceptable so long as the slab has not been sealed with material that's incompatible with the adhesive. You can tell if a slab has been sealed by dropping a bit of water on it. If the water beads up, the slab has probably been sealed. Because there's no practical way to tell if the sealer is compatible with the adhesive, you should remove it, by sanding or with a solvent. Depending on the sealer, a solvent like denatured alcohol, paint thinner, lacquer thinner or acetone should work.

Moisture control is a concern throughout the life of a wood floor. Obviously, a soaking with liquid water will do serious damage. Just as damaging, albeit slower, is moisture seeping up through the subfloor from an improperly vented crawl space. The flooring may swell more than the expansion gaps you've provided will allow. Although they might not buckle, the boards will probably push so forcefully against each other that they'll suffer compression damage. Come drier weather, the wood won't expand again, and large gaps will show.

Figure 10 on p. 49 shows a well-designed crawl space. Exposed soil in the crawl space should be covered with 6-mil plastic while the space itself should have adequate ventilation around the perimeters. Slabs should have adequate drainage beneath and around their perimeters and should be sealed on their outer face. In addition, below-grade or on-grade slabs should be sealed with a hydrostatic sealer to prevent moisture from creeping into the flooring installed on its surface. In very cold climates, to avoid frozen pipes and excess heat loss, the vents can be blocked during the winter. Also, to improve their effectiveness, insulating batts between floor joists should have an airspace rather than be stuffed against the subfloor.

Underlayment

Most people attempting their first wood floor are utterly confused about underlayment. And with good reason. There are so many types of wood flooring today that it's hard to know when to use underlayment and when not. Floating plank floors, for instance, can be laid over just about anything, including low-pile carpet, exposed aggregate and even another hardwood floor.

When should you use underlayment? First, the easy ones: install a minimum of ½-in. underlayment when whatever defects your subfloor has can't be corrected. I always install at least ½ in. of underlayment for a parquet

Figure 11 **Underlayment**

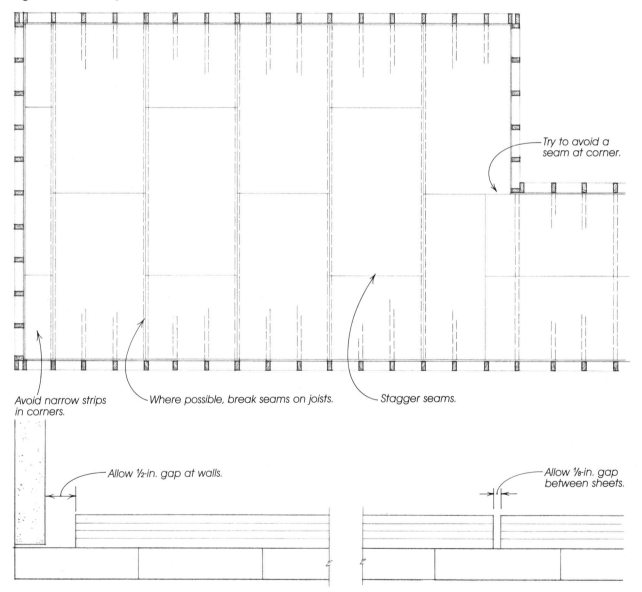

Try to avoid a seam at corner.

Avoid narrow strips in corners.

Where possible, break seams on joists.

Stagger seams.

Allow ½-in. gap at walls.

Allow ⅛-in. gap between sheets.

floor installed over most subfloors, except concrete. Where possible, I'll use ¾-in. thick plywood.

Parquet can be glued directly to concrete if necessary. A solid strip or plank floor can be installed directly over concrete in a thick bed of adhesive, although I don't generally do it. It's usually best to go to a laminated strip or plank product if you must glue directly to a slab. Whenever possible I advocate a minimum of ¾-in. underlayment (1⅛ in. is preferred) to provide nailing purchase and to even out undulations in the slab. Plywood can be rawl pinned or fastened with powder-actuated fasteners. Gluing also works well and may be necessary when sandwiching a layer of sound-deadening material between the slab and the plywood. If you do use an adhesive, make sure the slab is clean, dry and flat.

If the slab is very light or you're dealing with a subfloor that will transmit sound, put down a layer of cork or sound-deadening foam such as QuietCore (see the Resource Guide on p. 135). The foam can be glued or just laid on top of the slab. Next, install two layers of ½-in. ACX plywood over the foam, staggering the layers so the seams in the first layer are overlapped by the second layer. The two layers should be fastened together by ¾-in. or ⅞-in. screws that don't penetrate the foam, thereby preserving its sound-proof integrity.

As long as strip or plank flooring can be laid across the joists without worry about deflection and assuming that there is a good nailing surface, underlayment is not necessary. If you really want to rule out any deflection and creaking, install a layer of ¾-in. ACX plywood. If laying your flooring perpendicular to the joists would make the room look odd or just isn't what you had in mind, install a layer of underlayment.

If you don't want to spend the time and money on underlayment, one compromise is to lay the flooring on the diagonal so it gets good support from the joists. Diagonal patterns, however, can be visually overwhelming, especially in small rooms. It doesn't make sense to live with an annoying pattern just to save a little money on underlayment. Another consideration is the height gain the underlayment will create. Measure this against the effort and expense. Reducers will match a higher floor to a lower one (see Figure 9 on p. 47), but some people don't like the looks of them and would prefer to have the flooring run in a different direction to avoid them.

If underlayment is necessary, I recommend ½-in. or ¾-in. exterior plywood with one good face (ACX) preferably tongue-and-groove. Use ½-in. ACX where height gain is a problem and ¾-in. ACX where it's not. Particleboard and hardboard are sold as underlayment, but I don't use them because they don't hold fasteners well and swell badly when exposed to moisture. A hardwood floor might itself survive a water trauma, providing that the flood is cleaned up quickly. But if it floods over a particleboard subfloor, you can expect big problems.

Figure 11 shows the general principles for installing underlayment. When it's convenient, break the sheets on joists and stagger the end seams. I like to nail underlayment with 8d or 10d ring-shank nails driven into the joists, whose positions can be marked on the underlayment with chalklines. Gluing underlayment with construction adhesive is optional, but will certainly reduce squeaks. Whether the underlayment will be glued or not, I cut and fit all of the sheets before fastening them to the subfloor. That way, I can find and correct any problems without having to remove the sheets I've already installed.

Recommended Underlayments for Tongue-and-Groove Hardwood Flooring				
	Random-length strip		Shorts (18 in. or less)	Square-edge strip
Orientation of flooring	up to 3¼ in. wide, ¾ in. thick	4 in. to 8 in. wide, ¾ in. thick	up to 3 in. wide, ¾ in. thick	1 in. to 3 in. wide, ½ in. to ⁵⁄₁₆ in. thick
Strips running at 90° to joists set 16 in. o.c.*	¾-in. T&G ACX plywood	⅞-in. T&G plywood, 1-in. square-edge plywood, or two layers of ½-in. ACX with staggered seams	1-in. T&G plywood or square-edge plywood	1⅛-in. T&G plywood or square-edge plywood
	¾-in. square-edge plywood	⅞-in. square-edge plywood	Two layers of ½-in. square-edge plywood with staggered seams	Two layers of ⅝-in. square-edge plywood with staggered seams
	¾-in. by 6-in. to 8-in. plank or shiplap laid diagonally or two layers of ½-in. square-edge plywood with staggered seams	¾-in. by 6-in. to 8-in. plank or shiplap laid diagonally or two layers of ½-in. square-edge plywood with staggered seams		
Strips diagonal or with joists set 16 in. o.c.*	1⅛-in. T&G plywood, or two layers of ⅝-in. square-edge plywood with staggered seams Bridging between joists			

*For joists set 24 in o.c., add ¼-in. underlayment; for joists set 12 in. o.c., subtract ⅛-in. underlayment.

Figure 12 **Plywood-on-Slab and Screed Systems**

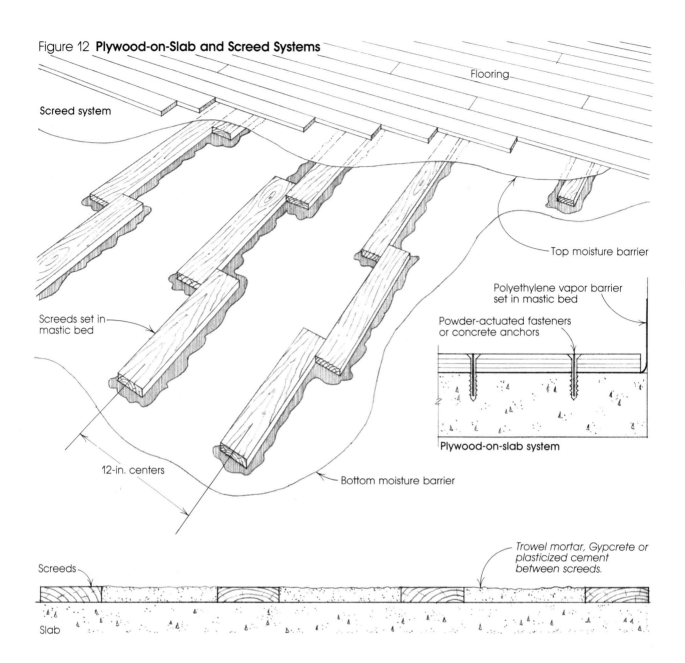

Flooring

Screed system

Top moisture barrier

Polyethylene vapor barrier
set in mastic bed

Powder-actuated fasteners
or concrete anchors

Screeds set in
mastic bed

Plywood-on-slab system

12-in. centers

Bottom moisture barrier

*Trowel mortar, Gypcrete or
plasticized cement
between screeds.*

Screeds

Slab

Plywood-on-slab and screed systems

As I explained earlier, parquet, laminated strip and plank, and floating plank systems are the only kinds of flooring that should be applied directly to concrete slabs. Conventional strip and plank over concrete will have to be fastened to plywood underlayment or solid-wood screeds. The plywood-on-slab method is basically just another form of underlayment.

To create a vapor barrier that will protect both the underlayment and finish flooring from moisture, cover the slab with 4-mil to 6-mil polyethylene, as shown in Figure 12. First, lay a bed of adhesive on the slab. Then roll the poly into it. The plastic should be large enough to overlap the baseboards. The excess can be trimmed later. Next, install underlayment as described above. Regular masonry nails or concrete fasteners will do, but powder-actuated fasteners are easier and faster, even if you have to rent the tool. In any case, be certain the plastic is sealed at the seams (a 6-in. overlap should be sufficient) and that the plywood is flat.

Fasten the sheets in the center first, then work toward the edges of each sheet. If you use lead or sleeve-type concrete anchors, I suggest pouring a small amount of asphalt mastic or construction adhesive into each hole to prevent water seepage. Another vapor-barrier method (or when working over lightweight concrete) is to score the back of the underlayment with a 12-in. grid ½ in. deep, then bed the sheets in a coat of cut-back asphalt mastic troweled onto the slab. Use an adhesive that will remain fairly elastic over time, such as a "cold-tar" mastic. By "cut back," I mean an asphalt adhesive that has been thinned somewhat with the appropriate solvent, generally paint thinner. Trowel the mastic evenly over the entire slab, then allow it to set for 12 hours or longer before laying the underlayment.

Screeds are another common way of setting a wooden floor over a slab. Screeds are basically treated 1x3s or 1x4s over which strip or plank flooring is laid. They provide a nailing surface and keep the flooring from direct contact with the slab, thereby reducing moisture exchange.

As shown in Figure 12, screeds are set in a mastic bed between two layers of polyethylene vapor barrier. Fastening the screeds to the slab is optional. It's acceptable just to bed them in mastic on top of the lower vapor barrier.

If you do decide to fasten the screeds to the slab, use powder-actuated fasteners or concrete anchors. I use pressure-treated 1x3s or 1x4s for the screeds. Lay the first layer of plastic, spread the mastic and place the screeds on 9-in. centers for strip and plank flooring up to 4 in. wide. In order to have adequate nailing surface, flooring wider than 4 in. will require a subfloor over the screeds or plywood-on-slab underlayment.

Now and then, I encounter a slab with an embedded radiant-heat system, in which case I trowel mortar, Gypcrete or plasticized cement between the screeds, flush with their tops, as shown in Figure 12. Once set, the mortar can be sanded flush to the screeds. Besides providing additional support for the flooring, the mortar adds thermal mass for the heating system.

Another version of the screed and radiant heat system that's a popular retrofit method consists of 2x4s installed on 9-in. to 12-in. centers on top of the slab. The radiant coils are are intertwined between and around these then covered with another layer of concrete, Gypcrete or other heavy-mass substance. The flooring is then nailed to the screeds or to ¾-in. plywood underlayment installed over the screeds.

In the early days of radiant heat, home owners typically cranked the systems up to 110°F or more, which broke down the adhesives and caused glued-down flooring to loosen. These days, radiant heat systems are more carefully regulated and adhesives are better, but the constant warming and cooling of the floor will loosen up fillers over time, causing them to pop out. This argues for strip, plank or parquet with eased edges or V-grooves as the best finish floor over a radiant slab. V-grooved or eased-edged flooring is not generally filled after installation, and it helps hide the inevitable gaps between boards or pieces that develop from being installed over radiant systems. It's thus more resistant to the demands placed upon it by a radiant system.

Once the initial courses have been laid and aligned, the strips can be fastened with a power nailer, a tool that drives and sets a barbed floor nail.

Strip and Plank:
Layout and Installation

Chapter 4

Compared to the mundane tasks of buying materials and preparing the subfloor, the actual process of laying a hardwood floor usually goes very quickly. And despite the inevitable minor problems, the work is quite gratifying. Even after 15 years in the flooring business, I still get a kick out of seeing a shabby subfloor transformed into a warm, inviting surface as course after course of flooring is nailed down.

If you've done careful prep work, you will have anticipated (and corrected) the subfloor's defects. It will take a few hours to develop an efficient work rhythm, but once you do, the flooring will go down quickly and smoothly. Minor kinks in layout and installation are unavoidable, however, so in this chapter, in addition to the fundamentals, I'll explain some tricks of the trade for correcting problems on the fly.

Actual installation happens in two stages: design and layout, followed by racking, cutting, fitting and nailing. Of the two, the design-and-layout stage is surely the more perplexing, especially for beginners. Some people have a natural knack for good floor design, but those who don't shouldn't find the task insurmountable so long as they're willing to spend a few hours with a sketch pad and tape measure before installing the first board.

As far as design and installation go, strip and plank flooring are virtually identical, so nearly all of the information given here applies to both types. However, there are some minor differences, which the chapter's final section will examine.

Strip and plank design

As I explained in Chapters 1 and 2, the particular look your floor will have depends on the type of flooring (strip or plank), species, pattern, direction of layout and finish. In Chapter 1, I discussed some floor selection criteria without regard to pattern or layout design. But manipulation of pattern has a dramatic effect on final appearance. Even ordinary oak strip flooring can lend itself to a wide aesthetic range simply by changing the direction in which the strips are laid. But as you'll soon find out, the pattern that looks best sometimes won't work for structural or other reasons, so you'll have to compromise your way to the second or third choice. The art of designing floors is to make the most of what will work rather than to force the ideal design into the wrong application.

To the uneducated eye, the work of an expert floor mechanic may appear perfect, even though the room may not be. The strips or planks will run in the best-looking direction possible, given the constraints of the subflooring and walls. There will be no obvious runouts or tapers, and headers and borders will appear to be balanced. In fact, a good mechanic will have manipulated the layout so that the most visible parts of the floor—what I call the focal points—will appear perfect, while problem areas will have been subdued or subtly fixed in the less conspicuous corners. This sort of compromise is unavoidable because no room in any house—at least none that I've encountered—is perfectly square, level, flat and plumb.

A room can have one or several focal points, depending on its size and shape and how many entrances there are. A focal point is what the eye settles on first when you enter the room. It's also the area where you want the straightest rows and the tightest joints. It could be a fire-

Figure 13 **Focal Points**

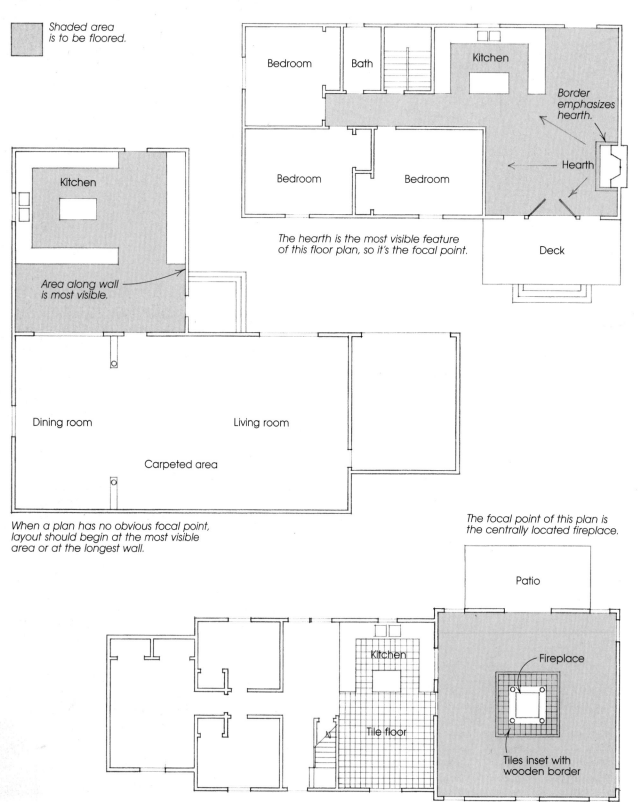

Shaded area is to be floored.

Kitchen

Bedroom Bath Kitchen

Border emphasizes hearth.

Bedroom Bedroom

Hearth

Deck

The hearth is the most visible feature of this floor plan, so it's the focal point.

Area along wall is most visible.

Dining room Living room

Carpeted area

When a plan has no obvious focal point, layout should begin at the most visible area or at the longest wall.

The focal point of this plan is the centrally located fireplace.

Patio

Kitchen

Fireplace

Tile floor

Tiles inset with wooden border

Mitered borders (above) and headers (below), both combined with inlay, accent the floor's focal point. Headers are also a good solution where strip floors running perpendicular to each other must meet.

place hearth, a door threshold, a group of cabinets, an open expanse of floor, a long hallway and so on.

Figure 13 shows some examples. The idea is to center the design (and layout) around the focal points, making them as appealing as possible. The floor layout then commences at the focal points and proceeds toward less noticeable areas, where any problems can be discreetly dealt with.

Borders and headers are frequently used by floor mechanics to highlight focal points. A border is like a picture frame that wraps the focal point. It's often a wider section of flooring, and can be mitered or lap jointed at the corners. The main field of the flooring butts to the border. Lesser features such as heating or cooling registers, island walls and stairwell openings can also be bordered.

One type of layout is called a picture frame. In this design, you border an entire cabinet line or every wall in every room throughout the entire installation. I like to use borders as often as possible because they're simple but also unusual enough to give my floors a distinctive character, especially if combined with inlay, as described in the sidebar on pp. 66-67.

Figure 14 **Flooring Direction**

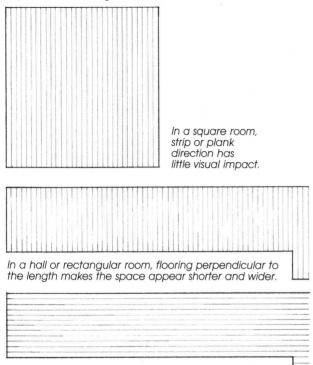

In a square room, strip or plank direction has little visual impact.

In a hall or rectangular room, flooring perpendicular to the length makes the space appear shorter and wider.

Flooring parallel to the length makes the space appear longer and narrower.

Flooring laid diagonally can make a room look larger, but may appear chaotic in a small room.

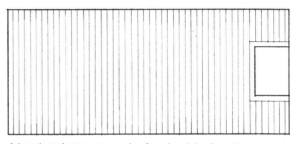

A bordered area around a focal point often determines the starting point. Layout generally proceeds from the border into the rest of the room.

A header is a piece of flooring that's usually (but not always) placed at right angles to the regular run of flooring. Headers are commonly used as a visual buffer between two floors whose strips run in the same or opposite directions or at changes in flooring material. Headers are not just a cosmetic treatment. They have a structural purpose as well, tying together the tongued ends of strips or planks. Tapered reducers and nosing pieces at the tops of stairs perform the same function as a header.

With species and type decided, the direction the strips or planks run is the most important consideration in floor design. In a square room with no obvious focal point, sufficient subflooring and underlayment and no borders, it doesn't much matter which way the floor runs. The primary consideration would probably be the direction the floor runs in relation to the main entry or how the floor looks when viewed through the door to an adjacent room. If the room were rectangular, running the strips or planks parallel to the length of the room will make it appear longer; running them perpendicular will have the opposite effect. The same is true in hallways. A long, narrow hallway will look wider if the flooring is run perpendicular to the hall's length.

A third alternative, diagonal layout, can make a room appear somewhat larger, but it may appear chaotic, too. Where borders will be used as focal points, design the border first, then decide on a direction for the rest of the floor. A diagonal layout can sometimes emphasize an adjacent room or adjoining area, particularly if the adjacent area runs parallel to the diagonal run of flooring.

Sometimes you won't have a choice on floor direction. It will be dictated by the subfloor and framing. So it will have maximum support, strip and plank flooring should always run perpendicular to the joists, unless you've installed a minimum of 1⅛ in. of plywood or plank underlayment. If that conflicts with your design, the only solution is to nail down the necessary underlayment and then run the flooring the way you want. However, besides adding expense and work, underlayment raises the finished floor's height, which means you'll have to make some adjustments in door casings, shorten a few doors and perhaps install reducers to match the higher floor to a lower one in an adjacent room. You may also have to remove and reinstall a weatherized exterior door and threshold.

At the very least, you are likely to end up with some troublesome floor-height changes in one or more doorways unless you install underlayment throughout all the rooms on the same level. So you have to ask yourself if the floor direction is worth the extra work.

An existing floor in an adjacent room can affect floor direction too. If the new floor will butt to an existing floor and run the same direction (assuming the same level) you can join the two with a dividing strip or header or "lace" the new floor into the old, as shown in the bottom photo on p. 57 and in Figure 26 on p. 80, respectively. Lacing in is a lot of work. I do it only when the customer insists, and I'm careful to point out that the color of the new flooring won't always match the old. A header is the easiest solution, but lacing usually results in better appearance, color variations notwithstanding.

To figure out how you want the floor to look, carefully measure the floor plan and draw it to scale on a piece of graph paper. Sketch in all of the details. You may want to determine the lack of squareness or alignment of opposing walls at this point, which may affect the layout. Pay particular attention to features that might make good focal points. With your floor plan in hand, walk into the room from various directions and make note of what areas or features you notice first.

In the floor depicted in the videotape, my living and dining room, I picked the fireplace as the focal point. As you can see in the first drawing in Figure 13 on p. 56, it's the dominant feature when you enter from either the hall, the kitchen or through a pair of glass sliders from the deck. The hearth is bordered with a 5-in. wide oak border with ebony and brass inlay. I also bordered the forced-air heat registers and fitted each with a custom hardwood grille. As the drawing shows, the strips run perpendicular to the car decking. This looks fine in the living and dining room, but I would have preferred to run the floor lengthwise down the hallway. This would have required underlayment, however, since running strip or plank the same direction as the car decking would not have been structurally sound. Time and budget constraints, coupled with my desire to match the heights of the new flooring to the existing flooring, argued against underlayment. So I bit the bullet and compromised.

So far, I've discussed only strip direction as a design variable. If you're willing to do the work, however, you can get dramatic results with ordinary strip or plank flooring by laying a pattern floor. Pattern floors can be simple borders around a section of flooring laid perpendicular to the main floor, or they can be very complex affairs, involving strips or planks of different width and species. Figure 15 shows some examples.

Before considering a pattern floor, be sure you have adequate subflooring to support it. Nothing looks worse than a bunch of gaping joints in an otherwise beautiful pattern. Patterns sometimes look best in formal or semi-formal settings. Dining-room floors, for example, are often patterned to establish a center for the dining table. Ordinary entryways or foyers can be enhanced with patterns designed to reflect the architectural sense of the rest of the house. Log-cabin corners convey a traditional feeling;

Figure 15 **Pattern Floors**

Tile, marble or lighter/darker wood

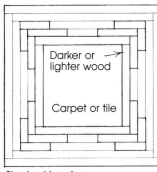

Darker or lighter wood

Carpet or tile

Stacked border

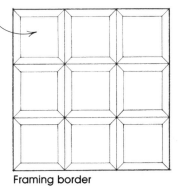

Framing border

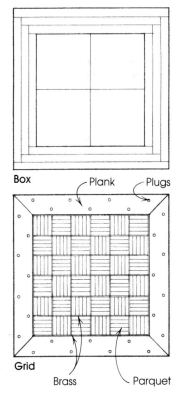

Plank   Plugs

Box

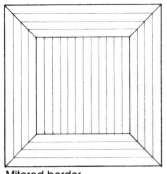

Mitered border

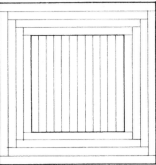

Traditional log-cabin bordered room

Grid

Brass   Parquet

mitered corners look more modern. Parquet can be effective inside a border of strip or plank in entries, dining rooms and living rooms. One of my favorite designs is marble or carpet surrounded by a border pattern of hardwood flooring.

Layout

As I explained in Chapter 3, the perfect room doesn't exist. No matter how carefully the carpenters built the frame, settling and wood movement are facts of life. Besides knocking the floor out of level, settling (or framing errors at the outset) may result in an out-of-square room. The process of layout is an attempt to compensate for these problems. Out-of-squareness is rarely a major problem. Like level and plumb, it's a relative value. As Figure 16 shows, depending on the floor direction, out-of-squareness can sometimes be ignored.

But when a floor plan looks like a trapezoid or if two adjacent rooms are out of square to each other, you'll have to take corrective action, either at layout before the first course is laid or by tapering individual strips during installation to disguise runout. It's not uncommon to spend as much as one-third of the entire job sizing up the subfloor and determining the layout of the first few courses.

The real culprit is not so much out-of-square as it is out-of-parallel. This condition is most noticeable in halls or long, narrow rooms. It may take a lot of head scratching, but these errors are best dispersed gradually rather than all at once at some conspicuous spot. Most floor installers use the baseline method to correct errors to keep the floor running true. A baseline is a fixed datum determined by the installer, a reference point from which all the courses of flooring are measured. The baseline usually parallels the longest wall or, in a room with walls of equal length, it should parallel the most visible wall or the primary focal point.

The baseline's parallelism can be fudged to take up errors, in which case it's called a balanced baseline. If there are no errors (an unlikely eventuality) or if they're too small to worry about, it's called a simple baseline. Let's consider the simple baseline first. In this case, we're assuming the room is nearly square and that the opposite wall is nearly parallel. I realize that "nearly" is a fuzzy qualifier. How much is too much? If the out-of-parallel error is less than ¼ in. per 6 ft. of wall run, I usually don't worry about it. If it's more than that, the simple baseline won't work. To establish the simple baseline, measure out from the wall 1 ft. plus a distance equal to the face width of one flooring strip, plus the expansion gap, as shown in Figure 17.

Figure 16 **Checking for Square and Parallel**

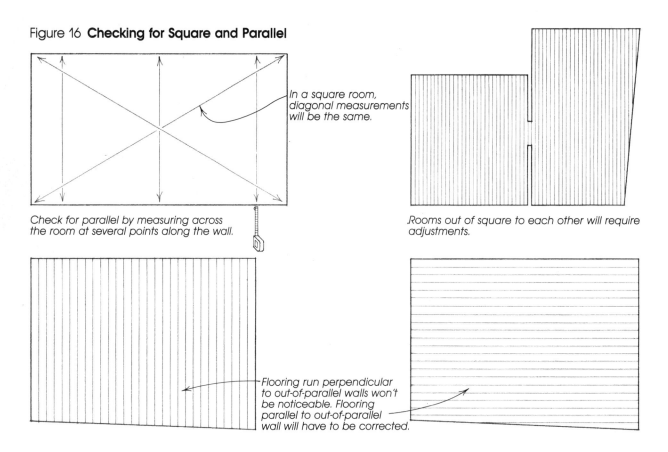

In a square room, diagonal measurements will be the same.

Check for parallel by measuring across the room at several points along the wall.

Rooms out of square to each other will require adjustments.

Flooring run perpendicular to out-of-parallel walls won't be noticeable. Flooring parallel to out-of-parallel wall will have to be corrected.

Figure 17 **Simple and Balanced Baselines**

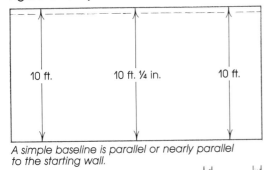

A simple baseline is parallel or nearly parallel to the starting wall.

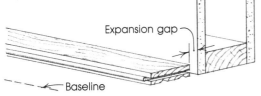

In lieu of a simple baseline, place removable shims or scraps of flooring between wall and strip to establish expansion gap.

A balanced baseline splits the out-of-parallel error across the width of the floor. Any remaining error is taken up evenly with tapered pieces, or at the opposite wall.

After checking that the walls are parallel, strike a balanced baseline on the subfloor.

At the opposite end of the wall, measure and mark again, then connect the two points with a chalkline. This is a simple baseline, and it serves as the guide for the first course. Minor out-of-parallel errors can be taken up later by a tapered strip or two at mid-floor or at the opposite wall line. When the walls are parallel, some floor mechanics dispense with the baseline entirely in favor of shims or scraps of flooring placed temporarily between the wall and the first course. These pieces are equal to the thickness of the expansion gap, and they serve to align the first course. This method is fast but you have to remember to sight down the strips to make sure that bows and dips in the wall aren't translated into a wavy layout.

Errors greater than ¼ in. per 6 ft. will have to dispersed to both sides of the room by the balanced-baseline method. Figure 17 shows how this is done. Let's say that the out-of-parallel error is 1 in. over the length of an 18-ft. wall. Start by measuring out from the walls at point A a distance of 14¾ in. (½ in. for the expansion gap, 2¼ in. for the width of the first course and 1 ft. of working space). At point B, measure again, this time adding ½ in. to your addition for a total of 15¼ in. Snap a chalkline connecting these points, and you have your balanced baseline. The ½ in. takes up half of the total error. The rest can be taken up later, either at the opposite wall or by tapering a few strips in the middle of floor, or by a combination of the two.

The first course of flooring will be positioned 1 ft. from the balanced baseline. The situation described above assumes that the runout is consistent along the entire wall. If it's not, you can fudge the baseline's position by measuring back from the opposite wall at several points. The balanced baseline should reflect an average of measurements connecting these points. If borders or headers will be near the first course where a lot of error is being taken up, it may be necessary to adjust the baseline slightly to keep the first course from being noticeably out of parallel with the border.

The baseline doesn't have to start on one wall or the other. It can be struck in the center of the room, as shown in Figure 18. This is a good solution if you want to lay in two directions at once on a very large floor or in a house that's "cut up" with a lot of rooms, walls, cabinets or other fixed features. Also, in a very wide room, starting in the center is a good way to minimize the effects of wood movement. Flooring tends to move toward the tongue, and if the tongues face in opposite directions starting in the center, the flooring will tend to shrink and swell from the center outward, rather than across the entire width of the floor. For this to work, the two center strips are placed back to back and mated to one another with a slip tongue

or spline, as shown in the drawing. Both the center rows are face nailed in place.

Problem layouts. When adjacent rooms are completely out of square with one another, you might consider installing headers dividing these rooms or running the flooring in opposing directions, assuming you have the correct subflooring and or underlayment to accomplish this. A diagonal layout is sometimes the only way to hide acute out-of-squareness.

Slight changes in floor level from room to room are often best handled by changing the direction of the flooring or by installing headers to turn what would otherwise be a defect into a decorative element. If you are confused about what to do in a difficult situation, dry lay a few square feet of flooring or sketch a scaled drawing to try out various ideas.

Figure 18 **Center Laying**

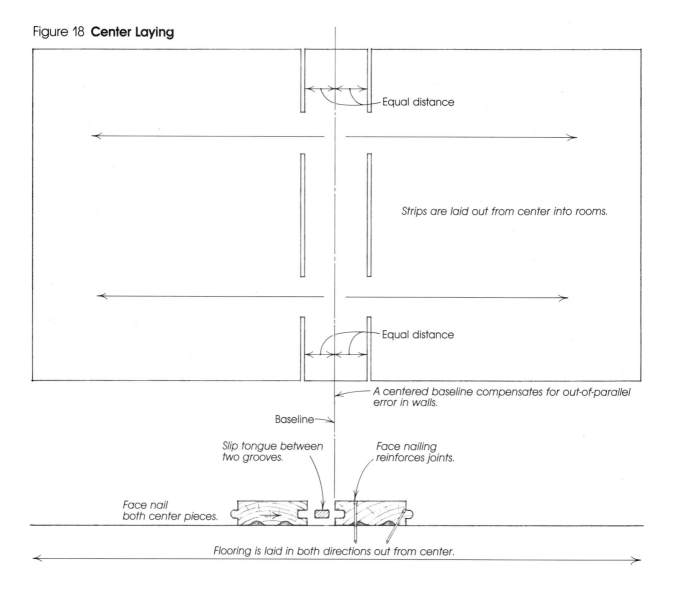

Equal distance

Strips are laid out from center into rooms.

Equal distance

A centered baseline compensates for out-of-parallel error in walls.

Baseline →

Slip tongue between two grooves.

Face nailing reinforces joints.

Face nail both center pieces.

Flooring is laid in both directions out from center.

Getting started

With prep, design and layout done, it's time to get down to business. Before nailing the first course, however, the subfloor should be covered with a vapor barrier. I recommend three-ply kraft building paper, but some floor installers use 15-lb. to 30-lb. builder's felt instead. Many of the commercial sound-deadening materials, such as GAF'S Quiet-Core, serve a dual purpose, effectively acting as both vapor barriers and sound insulation. I don't recommend polyethylene or other low-permeability materials immediately beneath the flooring. These restrict air movement and often produce condensation, causing the flooring to cup and thus defeating the entire purpose of the vapor barrier.

Always use a vapor barrier when installing a floor over an unheated space. It's optional over a heated space, but I recommend at least kraft paper to provide a clean working surface and to lessen squeaks. Simply staple the paper down as you go. Don't forget to transfer baselines to the face of the paper. While you're at it, mark any high or low spots in the subfloor that you were not able to correct. Try to position your strips to bridge these spots rather than having the butt ends break over them.

Three-ply kraft paper serves as a vapor barrier and pad for the finish flooring (above). Any dips or uncorrected high spots should be marked on the paper so strips can bridge them (below).

Borders are marked for cutting directly from the features they surround (left). In order to fit this border around rough mortar on the hearth, the author cut a rabbet in the back of the border (right).

I always try to start a floor by installing the borders, headers and nosings near the first course. These elements will get noticed whether they are focal points or not, so you want them to be as perfect as possible. If they're saved for last, the borders rather than the floors may have to absorb any unforeseen errors. As shown in the photos above and on the facing page, the border I used for the hearth consists of 5-in. wide plank flooring with a band of decorative inlay made from a combination of brass and ebony. The inlay process is described in the sidebar on pp. 66-67.

I made up the border in lengths a bit longer than I figured I'd need, to allow extra material for scribing and mitering the corners. The brick face of the hearth was relatively straight, but sometimes hearths are irregular or crooked. In these cases, you'd have to scribe the border to get a tight fit to the brick surface (Figure 19). Use a belt sander, block plane or rasp to trim to your scribed line. For this border, I fit the long piece first, then cut the miters with a chopsaw. The border is fastened to the subfloor with 2-in. No. 12 woodscrews driven into counterbored holes. Later, the counterbores will be plugged.

If you know wood flooring will be laid in a room where masonry hasn't yet been installed, you can have the mason hold the brickwork above the floor so the finish floor-ing can be inserted snugly into a space between the brick and the subfloor. Do this by installing a temporary border before the mason begins work. Once the masonry is done, remove the border and then slide the finish floor into the resulting groove.

When retrofitting next to masonry, I'll often leave a ⅛-in. gap to be filled later with clear silicone caulk. This catches the color of both materials to help blend them and it also allows space for the wood flooring to expand and contract against the unyielding brick or stone. If you want to disguise the joint, sprinkle a bit of dry mortar on the caulk while it's still wet.

On this floor, the heating registers are also bordered. I considered bordering the island wall that separates the kitchen from the living room, but later decided against it. In any event, all such borders can be set before the first course is nailed. They can also be installed later as the flooring advances toward them, but I find it more efficient to cut and loose fit all borders first. Temporarily tack down the across-the-room borders. Then, as you approach them with the main field of flooring, you can adjust as necessary.

If you want a really distinctive floor (and don't mind three times the work) border the room's entire perimeter. Figure 20 shows how this is done.

Flat-head, square-drive screws fasten the border to the subfloor. The holes will be filled with wooden plugs.

Figure 20 **Fitting to a Border**

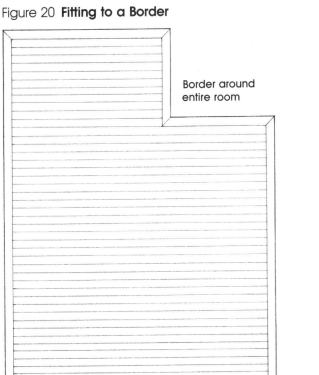

Border around entire room

Figure 19 **Scribing**

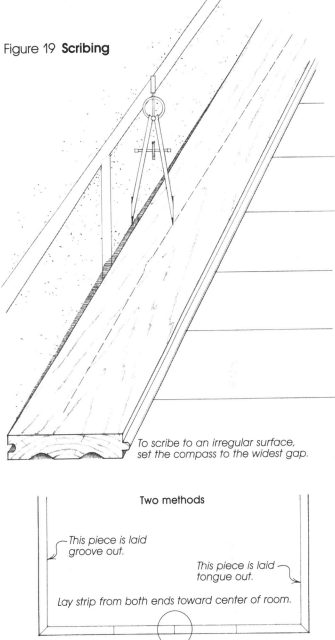

To scribe to an irregular surface, set the compass to the widest gap.

Two methods

This piece is laid groove out.

This piece is laid tongue out.

Lay strip from both ends toward center of room.

Where two strips meet, back-bevel and face nail...

...or install slip tongue or spline where strips meet in center of floor.

Decorative Inlays

Soon after I got into the hardwood-flooring business, I began to look for ways to set my floors apart from those of my competitors. One method that I have used with good results is decorative inlays of contrasting wood or metal. Inlay is a relatively easy and inexpensive way of dressing up what would otherwise be a rather ordinary wood floor.

By definition, inlaying is the process of insetting one material into another. Sometimes a groove or channel is created to house the inlay, but in my opinion, this method is not nearly as stable for floor use as is using an inlay material equal to the thickness of the finish flooring. In that sense, what I do is not strictly inlay, since I build the materials right into the floor as it's

being laid. Unlike traditional inlay, which is usually thinner than the host material, my inlay is as thick as the flooring itself.

One of my favorite techniques is to apply thin bands of metal and exotic wood to the edges of borders or headers, as shown in the photo below right. These thin lines of color contrast sharply with the surrounding flooring and are real eye-catchers. Another popular design with clients is what I call the grid. This is a geometric pattern (frequently square or rectangular) of parquet flooring bordered by metal trim and inlaid into a regular plank or strip floor. The grid is a nice touch in an entryway or as an island in the middle of a kitchen or dining room.

To make border inlay, first select the wood and metal you'd like to use. I prefer brass or aluminum because they're soft, easy to cut and can usually be sanded without showing a lot of scratching and without tearing up the sanding belts, as harder metals tend to do. Some caution is advised here. Wood and metal have different coefficients of expansion and contraction. Wood moves as it picks up and gives off moisture, while metals change dimension with temperature changes. What this means is that metal in an inlaid floor will sometimes stand slightly above or below the wood surface, creating subtle ridges or grooves. There's really no way to avoid this, and I've found that it's usually not objectionable.

The decorative inlay shown below, a Greek key, is built up as the floor is laid. The inlay is the same thickness as the surrounding flooring. At right, walnut inlay frames a full-room border.

Buy bar stock about ¹⁄₁₆ in. to ¼ in. thick and as wide as the flooring is thick. If you have to cut the bar stock, brass and aluminum can be safely sawn on a bandsaw fitted with a metalcutting blade. Ebony, rosewood, padauk, purpleheart, walnut, cherry, mahogany and maple make nice inlay woods, although you could use any species with the color contrast you like. Saw the wood into strips that look good with the metal you intend to use.

I recommend developing patterns from scraps of wood and metal the actual size you plan to use. These can be dry laid in test patterns. You might even apply finish to see how the various metals and wood will look together—some woods tend to bleed onto the metal during sanding. For border inlay, I make up the border and inlay in lengths slightly longer than I think I'll need.

The inlay is fastened to the edge of the border with brads, as shown in the photos at right. The nail holes must be predrilled with a bit slightly smaller than the nail's shank diameter. Clamp the inlay to the border piece, drill on about 4-in. centers, and nail. You might think that epoxy would be a better way to fasten the inlay. It will work, but beware: the heat of subsequent sanding and/or wood movement may break the bond, and there's no easy way to fix the joint if it opens up.

Once the inlay is attached to the border, you can fit it as described on p. 64. A chopsaw fitted with a carbide blade will cut the metal cleanly, although the cut may need a little touchup with a file or sandpaper to remove metal burrs. Later, when the floor is sanded, a little touchup with fine (150-grit) sandpaper will remove the most obvious scratching.

Inlays don't necessarily have to follow a border pattern; they can take on a shape of their own. Using a thin metal inlay around squares of parquet creates a nice effect. This approach requires an extremely rigid and flat underlayment, since parquet tends to deflect more than a strip or plank floor. The subflooring/underlayment combination should be at least 1½ in. thick and set on joists 16 in. on center or closer. Because ⁵⁄₁₆-in. parquet is too thin to edge nail, I recommend a

flexible epoxy adhesive for the metal and a solvent-based adhesive for the parquet. To hold the metal in place while the epoxy sets, tack a metal fence temporarily to the floor and use wedges to clamp the joint.

Border patterns made from combinations of different species are still done now and again, although their heyday was during Victorian times. Greek keys or French knots consist of full-thickness patterns inlaid into a strip or plank floor. These are more readily done in square-edge

flooring that can be face nailed or glued. Tongue-and-groove strips complicate the procedure.

The Greek key shown in the photo at left on the facing page was made up of individual pieces of contrasting wood, and the field of flooring was laid up to the pattern. If you really want a durable pattern, rather than face nailing, install slip tongues or splines into grooves cut in both the pattern wood and the flooring field. This requires a lot of extra work, but it will pay off in a stronger joint.

Combination wood and metal inlay should be made up in strips and attached to the flooring or borders on site, with brads (below). Bore a hole slightly smaller than the brad's diameter (bottom).

The first course

Before you start laying the floor, arrange all the tools you'll need in front of you, in the direction the floor will advance. If you will be laying the flooring away from an open area that has adequate space for you and your tools, you can save yourself some cleaning time by placing your saws behind you opposite your starting point. Now open up several bundles of flooring and sort through all the pieces to find enough straight strips for two starter rows and four finishing rows. The starter rows will be used right away, but save the finishing rows for later. Don't settle for any but the straightest stock. It's hard enough getting accurate starting and finishing rows without having to fight warped material.

Although it really doesn't matter which end of the wall you start with, right-handers will probably find it easiest to work from left to right, left-handers the opposite. Set the first strip with the tongue facing away from the starting wall in the direction you want to lay out the floor. Align the board with the baseline, as shown in the photo below. Don't forget to leave an expansion gap. It should be at least ½ in. If this isn't possible, you may want to undercut your drywall so the flooring can expand beneath it.

With the power nailer or by hand, face nail the first strip on 8-in. centers or closer, taking care that it doesn't slip off the baseline as the nails are driven. Start in the middle of the strip's length and work toward both ends. If your subflooring and underlayment together are less than 1¼ in. thick, you'll want to drive nails or fasteners through the finish boards and into joists wherever possible.

To locate the first course, measure back from the baseline (below), then face nail the first strip. Once you are three or four courses from the wall, there will be room for a side nailer. The tool shown in the photo above is a pneumatic model.

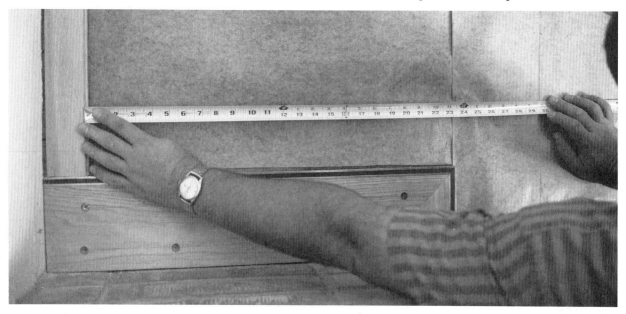

Floor fasteners shown at right include barbed nails for the power nailer (top and right), a ring-shank nail for underlayment, a cut nail (center) and a square-drive screw and wooden plugs for borders. The dark screw is a self-threading trim screw for fastening baseboards and casings.

Power-driven fasteners are barbed nails with a hooked head, as shown in the photo above. The barbs improve holding power, and since they're well-supported by the power nailer, the nails don't bend. Be certain all face-nail heads are set at least ⅛ in. below the surface. Later, these holes will be filled. An alternative to nailing the first course is to screw and plug it. It's more work, but some people prefer plugs to wood filler. The chart below gives the nailing schedule for various types of flooring.

Continue the first course along the entire length of the baseline, checking frequently as you nail for the row's continued alignment with the baseline. All end joints should be tight, with virtually no evidence of gapping. Hairline gaps, if unavoidable, can be filled later. You'll occasionally find boards or strips that don't match precisely. If the resulting crack is minor, you can leave it to be filled, but major variations should be dealt with by exchanging the defective board for a better-fitting one. When

Nail Schedule			
	Type of flooring	Fasteners	Spacing
Strip T&G	⅜ x 1½ ⅜ x 2	1¼-in. machine-driven fasteners, or 4d or 5d bright casing nails or finish nails	8 in. o.c. or closer
	½ x 1½ ½ x 2	1½-in. to 1¾-in. machine-driven fasteners, or 5d or 6d cut-steel or finish nails	8 in. to 10 in. o.c. or closer
	¾ up to 3¼ strip	2-in. machine-driven fasteners or cut nails, or 7d or 8d flooring nails	8 in. to 10 in. o.c. or closer
Plank T&G	¾ up to 4	2-in. machine-driven fasteners or cut nails, or 7d or 8d flooring nails	8 in. o.c. into and between joists or closer
	¾ x 4 and wider	2-in. machine-driven fasteners plus cut nails, or screw and plug to subfloor on planks wider than 4 in.	8 in. o.c. into and between joists or closer
Square-edge flooring	⁵⁄₁₆ x 1½	1-in. to 1¼-in., 15-ga. fully barbed flooring brads	2 nails, 7 in. o.c.
	⁵⁄₁₆ x 2	1 in. to 1¼-in., 15-ga. fully barbed flooring brads	5 in. o.c. on alternate sides of strip

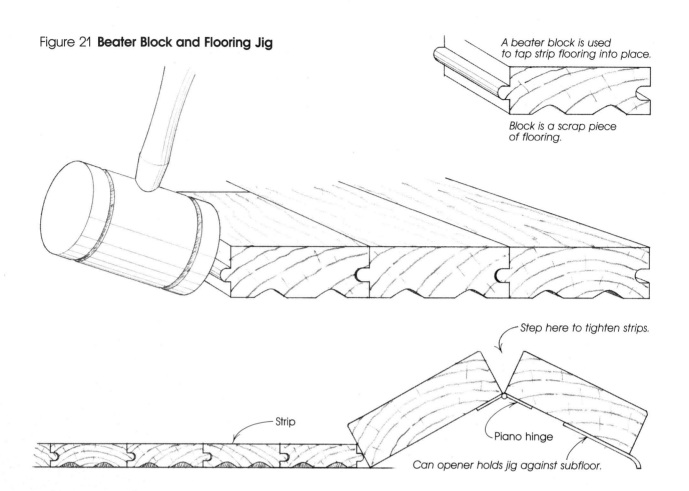

Figure 21 **Beater Block and Flooring Jig**

A beater block is used to tap strip flooring into place.

Block is a scrap piece of flooring.

Step here to tighten strips.

Strip

Piano hinge

Can opener holds jig against subfloor.

the problem is confined to the end of one board, saw the end off square and use it to start or end a row. Once the entire first row has been face nailed, I'll usually blind nail it as well, by hand if necessary, for additional strength.

Before going on, sight down the tongue side of the first row to see that the course is straight. Any kinks or dips you spot will be telegraphed to the next course. Try to tap them straight with a hammer and beater block, a small scrap of flooring whose groove fits over the tongue. Another method for aligning floor boards is to use the jig shown in Figure 21. A favorite method among some floor mechanics is to pull boards into alignment with a prybar or screwdriver. Unless there is a tight fit to a header, border or some other focal point, row ends should have at least ¼ in. or more of expansion gap.

For the second course, select strips whose lengths will result in the end joints being offset at least 3 in. Check this by laying the strips loosely in place. As you move down each row, tap each piece into place with a rubber mallet or a scrap block. Be careful not to dent or crumble the edges or ends of boards when doing this. Each piece should fit tightly against its neighbor with the tongue firmly seated in the grooves. This and future rows should be blind nailed through the tongue.

Depending on the width of the flooring and the kind of power nailer, it may be possible to power nail the second row. If you don't have room or don't feel comfortable blind nailing by hand, go ahead and face nail the second and even third course. Use your beater board to tap the courses straight if sighting reveals any crookedness.

Power nailers are easy to use but require a little caution. To strike the nailer's plunger, use a nylon, rawhide, rubber or plastic-faced dead-blow mallet, not a steel-faced hammer, which may cause the plunger to spall off bits of metal. Always wear safety glasses. The nails are well shielded by the nailer's mechanism and aren't likely to shatter, but due to the force behind the blow, bits and pieces of wood or metal can ricochet from the nailing surface. When face nailing, make sure the nailer is seated. Hit the plunger with a strong, single blow rather than a series of lighter taps. Some models of power fasteners allow you to drive a nail with a single blow or a series of blows. These can jam, however, leaving you with half-driven nails or two nails in the same hole.

The blind nailer's plate fits snugly into the tongue at just the right angle. A single hammer blow should drive and set the nail. If it doesn't, set the nail by hand so its head is just below the tongue's surface.

Racking

Once the first two courses are down, fitting and nailing will proceed apace. By the third course, you'll want to start "racking," or laying out several rows of flooring ahead of you. Your goal should be to blend all of the colors, grains patterns and board lengths into a pleasing whole. Obviously, you could spend many hours doing this and still not achieve perfection. At the very least try to cull wildly off-color boards (unless of course you like them) and ones with slash grain that's already lifted.

When arranging pieces, try to make sure the butt end joints aren't aligned or in "H" or "staircase" patterns, as shown in Figure 22. Even in a random-length floor, expect to have a significant percentage of short pieces. Try to distribute these evenly throughout the floor. Closets and cross-hatched hallways make great dumping grounds for excessive shorts in your stock.

Figure 22 **Hs and Staircasing**

When racking a floor, avoid predictable patterns like Hs and staircasing.

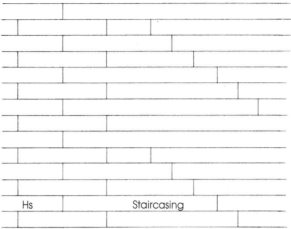

Hs   Staircasing

To rack a bundle of flooring, spread it out ahead of the work and sort the strips into pleasing grain and color patterns.

A long-handled screwdriver driven into the subfloor serves as a prybar to close open joints (left). Try to spot any wedged ends (right) before they're nailed down.

Working with nested bundles can help expedite the racking process. Most of the time, however, you'll be dealing with random-length bundles. Spread the strips out on the floor and move them around with your hands or feet. While you're sorting for length and color, look for any obviously defective pieces. Loose knots, worm holes, tapered pieces, planer and saw marks, fractured and splintered ends and tongues are all defects that shouldn't show up in graded flooring but occasionally do.

It's better to look carefully while you're racking and cull now than to pry the boards up later. If more than 5% of the strips in your order don't meet grade, you may be able to return that portion to the dealer for credit, less a handling fee. Be sure you have proof of the square footage purchased when returning the culled stock and that it has not be damaged or shows signs of nailing. Other defects that aren't normally subject to grading but that will still raise havoc in the finished floor are crooked boards, wedged ends and slash grain.

Crooked boards can sometimes be straightened with vigorous nailing through the tongues. Start nailing a crook in the center, then work to both ends. If it won't straighten, rip it out and saw out the straight portions for use elsewhere or discard it entirely. Minor crooks are the rule rather than the exception. To draw the joint home before nailing, use a long-handled screwdriver as a prybar. Drive

it into the subfloor near the middle of the strip and pry gently back on the tongue, then nail.

Wedged ends occur when the mill cuts the end match out of square. Sometimes, they run in groups in a bundle. If not culled, wedged ends result in unsightly gaps that can only be filled. You can salvage these pieces by using them at the start or end of courses where bad ends don't matter or can be cut off.

Slash grain is the floorman's misnomer for separation of the growth rings at or near the surface of the board. Sanding and finishing aggravate the separation, creating at the very least a hollow spot beneath the surface that may be fractured by a high heel. In severe cases, slash grain can lift up away from the surface in a splintering effect. Check each piece carefully for slash grain. If a slash-grained strip isn't spotted until it's too late, it can be mended by slicing open the loose piece of wood and gluing it back to the rest of the board. Sanding or scraping will smooth over the repair.

As the floor progresses, occasionally sight down the rows to check for straightness. Random-length strips will usually run straight, providing the first two courses are accurate. Shorts floors tend to get a little wavy, no matter how careful you are. Tap in the high spots with your beater block. If you can't fix the waviness, remove the offending strips or plan to shave a little wood off the next course or two with a plane. Shave the tongued edge above the tongue of the last nailed row or the grooved edge of the next course, tap the course home and sight it before nailing.

As with the end joints, the side matches should be tight, with only hairline gaps allowed. Minor variations in rows can be modified by the heft of your swing with the power-nailer mallet. Swing harder when nailing boards on the leading edge of bows in rows and just hard enough to drive and sink fasteners when nailing over low points.

Even for young installers, flooring is physically hard work. The up-down, down-up cycle gets tedious in a couple of hours. You can save a lot of wear on your back and knees by economizing your motions. Keep all of your tools positioned within a long arm's reach (or a short crawl) so you won't have stand up for each cut. I like to keep the chopsaw behind me and to my right. At first, it's on the subfloor. As soon as 10 or 15 courses are down, I put the chopsaw on the finished flooring, then clean up the mess I've made so the floor is uncluttered for racking and sorting. On a large floor, you might want to keep a chopsaw at both ends of the rows or press a circular saw into service where accurate cuts aren't important.

Continue advancing the floor, checking each course for tight joints and for overall straightness. Correct problems as they occur. As the butt end of each course nears the wall, mark its length for cutting by holding it in position, upside down, as shown in the photo below. Leave about a ¼-in. gap or more between the butt ends of the strips and the wall. This will make fitting easier and allow air circulation beneath the strips.

To preserve the end match when cutting strips to length, mark them in place, upside down.

Cutting and fitting

If all rooms were square or rectangular, laying a floor would be a cinch. But even simple floors have immovable objects—walls, cabinets, radiators, shelves, stairs and so on—around which the flooring must fit. As the advancing courses encounter these features, you'll have to trim around them. Trimming the flooring to fit along its length—ripping—is a common situation. It occurs because the courses rarely break evenly along a fixed feature. Occasionally, strips must be notched along their length so that objects can be "let into" the flooring. If

you're careful, you can measure the notches, but the easiest way is to scribe them directly, as we did to fit the strip around the hearth border. This is shown in the photos below and on the facing page.

The rip itself was done with a sabre saw equipped with a fine-tooth finishing blade. Note that the rip is back-beveled slightly to produce a tighter fit with the border (Figure 23). Don't overdo the bevel, however, or subsequent sanding will open up a gap. If the courses are running at a slight angle to the object you're fitting around, the rip cut has to be tapered. This can be done by trial and error or by scribing, as shown in Figure 19 on p. 65.

Rips and notches are also marked directly, as shown in the photos at right and on the facing page. To ease fitting chores, the rip is slightly back-beveled, as shown in Figure 23.

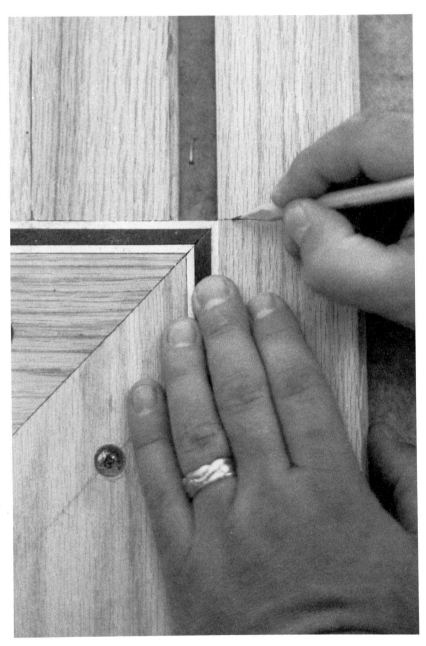

Strips that butt to fixed objects such as cabinets should be sawn flush to a tight fit if the joint will be visible or left with a gap if the joint will be covered by baseboard or otherwise won't be seen. If the cabinets haven't yet been set or can be conveniently removed, I try to run the flooring within 14 in. of the wall, leaving the ends "wild" or untrimmed. My first choice is to install, sand and finish flooring wall to wall under cabinets. This provides a better "seal" under cabinets and a flatter surface on which to set the cabinets. When given a choice, I will always lay flooring completely under island and L-shaped cabinets.

Figure 23 **Back-Beveling**

A slight back bevel makes for easier fitting.

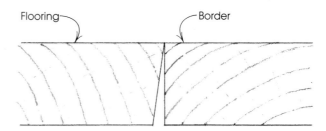

A slip tongue or spline slipped into the groove-to-groove joint where the strips meet a border strengthens what would otherwise be a weak line.

Butting to headers and borders. As shown in the photos above and on the facing page, borders and headers should be constructed so their tongues or grooves face their counterpart in the oncoming flooring. When in doubt, place their grooves facing out. The tongues of boards that join them can then lock into the grooves. Strong joints are important throughout the floor but are especially so along stretches where several boards butt into another piece of flooring, a border or a header. If there's no tongue-and-groove joint here, a so-called weak line will result. A weak line is susceptible to movement, causing the joints to open or be creaky.

You can almost always make a border or header with the groove out, but because the flooring end matches run in only one direction, you'll often have a groove-to-groove joint. It's tempting to just let it go at that and perhaps face nail the end of the boards. However, this results in ugly nail holes near a prominent feature and it also produces a weak line. To avoid this, the grooved end and edges can be locked together with a slip tongue or spline, as shown in Figure 24. For additional strength, I glue the joint with carpenter's glue or construction adhesive.

When you know that the grooved end of a row will be adjacent to a nosing, border or header, install the header with its tongue side out, then simply start each row at the header and lay in the opposite direction. If the border or whatever you're fitting to does not have a tongue or groove, you might consider using a router to mill a groove into it. This method is shown in Figure 24. It assumes that you have a slotting cutter and are able to precut the strips before installing them or that you can cut them in place.

Where a weak line is unavoidable, use the method shown in Figure 24 and apply adhesive to the subfloor near the joint. In this case, start the layout at the weak line and lay toward a wall or feature where the opposite ends of the courses can simply be butted.

If you have borders or headers on both ends of a row, you'll need to center-fit pieces in order to maintain your tongue-and-groove integrity along the weak line. This is done by first installing both ends of the same row using a tongue-and-groove or spline-in-groove method. The boards meet in the middle in a butt joint or, if you are ambitious, a spline-and-groove joint. If you use a butt joint, back-bevel the cut slightly to make for an easier fit.

To fit around borders and other fixed objects, the ends of strips can be notched.

Figure 24 **Border/Header Joints**

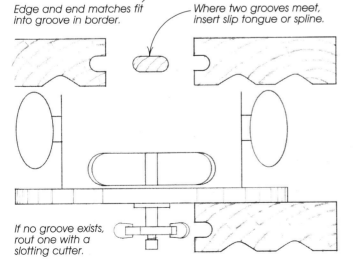

Border with groove out

Edge and end matches fit into groove in border.

Where two grooves meet, insert slip tongue or spline.

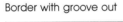

If no groove exists, rout one with a slotting cutter.

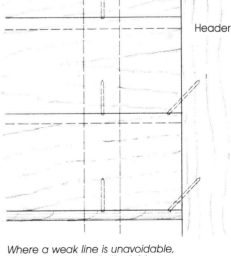

Header

Where a weak line is unavoidable, blind nail as close to the joist as possible and toenail into header.

Figure 25 **Nosings and Reducers**

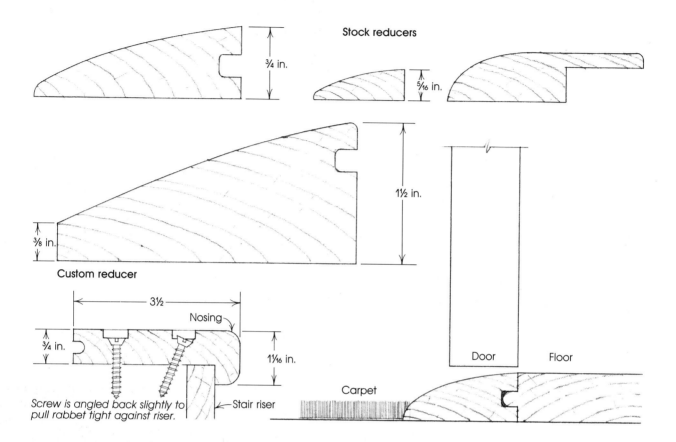

Stock reducers

¾ in.

⁵⁄₁₆ in.

1½ in.

⅜ in.

Custom reducer

3½

Nosing

¾ in.

1¹⁄₁₆ in.

Screw is angled back slightly to pull rabbet tight against riser.

←Stair riser

Door   Floor

Carpet

Stair nosing and reducers. The floor I laid for the videotape butts to a set of stairs ascending from a lower floor. Floor manufacturers make several sizes of nosing trim specifically for this situation. Figure 25 shows how the nosings are made and fastened. I drive two rows of screws into the nosing. The row nearest the front edge is slightly angled toward the top of the stair to draw the nosing's rabbet tight against the riser, as shown in the photos on the facing page.

As with the hearth border, the nosing has brass and ebony inlay so I couldn't cut a groove in it where the flooring butts. I used the weak-line nailing method described above. Note in the photos that the nosing was notched to fit around the wall and stair's skirtboard. When flooring goes from one level to another, a reducer is used, and it's handled much like a nosing in that it's cut to fit and screwed or nailed in place.

Reducers are available in several standard sizes, as shown in Figure 25, or you can make your own out of oak strip or plank flooring. When strip or plank flooring is used, be sure to remove the groove or tongue from the side opposite the floor. Tongues get in the way of other floor-covering materials, and grooves sometimes fracture

when subjected to heavy traffic. If a reducer is used between two rooms with a door or if it connects rooms with dissimilar flooring materials, position it as shown in Figure 25.

Backlaying and lacing in. As the floor advances, you'll inevitably encounter situations where you have to lay strips past an obstruction, then lay backward into a corner or an entire room. I had to do this for a closet in the floor depicted here. The obvious problem in backlaying is that there's no way to blind nail the tongue. In a closet, that's not so bad. You can fill in to the wall, then face nail it all in place. Once filled, these holes are not very obvious, particularly in the back of a closet.

Where the floor will be exposed, however, most floor mechanics like to "shoot a line" off the last row of flooring. One way of doing this is to dry lay a board from the last row extending past the wall or obstacle into the new room or area to be laid. Select a long, straight board for this and tap it snugly into place with its groove matched tightly to the tongue of the last board or two in the rows you've just finished. This becomes the baseline for the area to be backlaid.

The nosing piece that trims the top of stair was notched to fit around the wall (above). To pull it tight against the top riser, the forward row of screws was driven at a slight angle (below).

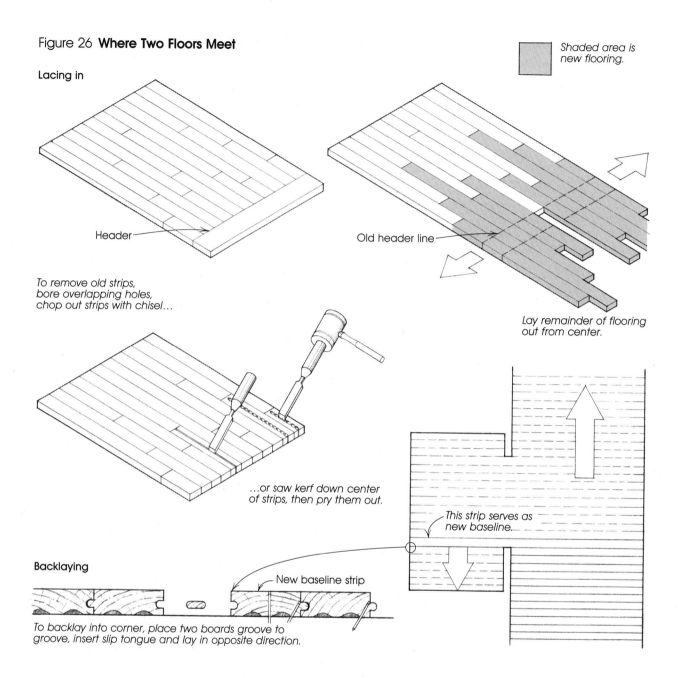

Figure 26 **Where Two Floors Meet**

Shaded area is new flooring.

Lacing in

Header

Old header line

Lay remainder of flooring out from center.

To remove old strips, bore overlapping holes, chop out strips with chisel...

...or saw kerf down center of strips, then pry them out.

This strip serves as new baseline.

Backlaying

New baseline strip

To backlay into corner, place two boards groove to groove, insert slip tongue and lay in opposite direction.

As shown in Figure 26, continue installing boards along your new baseline by face nailing until the row is completed. Next, position another row of strips with their grooves facing the grooves of the row you just installed. Insert a slip tongue between the two grooves, face nail the first row and then lay the flooring in the opposite of the direction you were originally going.

As I explained earlier in the book, the easiest way to match a new floor to an old one that runs in the same or a different direction is to install a header or reducer to which the old and new floor butt. This conveniently solves the problem of strip alignment for floors that run in

the same direction and into each other lengthwise. Because the old and new floors are separated by the header, color and grain contrast don't show as much.

Some clients insist on continuous flooring from one room to the next, in which case the new floor must be "laced into" the old one. To do this, strips of the old floor have to be removed, and the new floor laced in. This process is a lot easier with face-nailed square-edge flooring than with tongue-and-groove material. You can simply drive the nails completely through and lift the boards right out. With tongue-and-groove flooring it's a little more involved, as shown in Figure 26.

With any luck, the new strips will be the same width as the old, so you'll get tight joints. In the real world, they'll often be wider or narrower, in part from moisture changes but also because of milling variations. Even if the strips are the same size, internal pressures from years of moisture-induced wood movement causes boards to press tightly against one another. When you remove boards for lacing, you release this pressure, causing the floor to creep a little. Unless you work fast, and often even if you do, the same boards won't fit back into the space from which they've just been removed.

If the new strips are wider, trim the grooved sides and the leading edge of the tongue on its counterpart board with a plane. In extreme cases, deepen the groove slightly with a router or table-saw dado head. If the new strips are too narrow, make up wider ones from plank flooring or raw lumber. Establish a baseline using the laced-in pieces and their neighbors as your reference, and then lay flooring from the center out, as shown in Figure 26.

Often, an existing floor will be square to the room it's in but out of whack with the new adjacent floor. If you use the existing flooring as a reference point, the new flooring can come out looking pretty bad. In this instance, I recommend reversing the direction of the new floor and/or installing a header between the two rooms. If you must lace two such floors together, expect to spend a great deal of time trimming the edges of boards to create a bit of a "twist or turn" where the two floors meet so that some semblance of alignment can be achieved.

There is one other thing to consider when blending new wood with old. Time changes the apparent color of wood, particularly the more it's exposed to sunlight. Some of this color variation can be sanded away, but don't count on it. One way of avoiding the problems is to rob some pieces from a closet or another area to fill in where you removed the old flooring, then worry about mating the two floors farther into the new adjacent area, where it will be less noticeable.

Finishing up

As you near the opposite wall, measure from the face of the advancing flooring at several points along the course. The advancing courses should be within ½ in. to ¾ in. of being parallel to the wall, depending on the length of the rows and the visibility of the wall line. Any error greater than that should be corrected by tapering the strips. If the strips will advance toward a header, border or nosing, you can often adjust these to take up some of the error.

The usual way of way to correct out of parallel is to take up the error gradually over several courses. If the error is 1 in., for example, you can taper ⅛ in. off eight courses to correct it. Or you could take ¹⁄₁₆ in. off 16 rows without having to modify the grooves of succeeding rows. To mark for the taper, position the strips and strike a line the entire length of the course on the groove edge (Figure 27). With a jointer or hand plane, taper to the line on each piece. Tapers of ⅛ in. or more require deepening the grooves so these boards will seat flush against the tongues of adjacent pieces. Before nailing, sight the tapered course for straightness.

Figure 27 **Fitting the Final Piece**

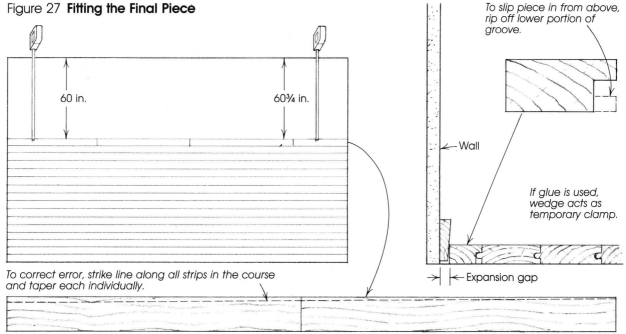

60 in.

60¾ in.

To correct error, strike line along all strips in the course and taper each individually.

To slip piece in from above, rip off lower portion of groove.

← Wall

If glue is used, wedge acts as temporary clamp.

→| |← Expansion gap

Another method is to correct the error all at once by tapering a course made of 3-in. plank. If the error is no more than 1 in., it shouldn't be too noticeable. Some floor mechanics correct a taper with a long, wedge-shaped piece when they get to the opposite wall. I don't like this method much because the baseboard gives the eye a nice straight edge to sight against, making the taper that much more obvious. I recommend that the tapered board be positioned at mid-room.

Pulling the walls. Once any errors have been corrected, the courses can be taken right to the opposite wall. As you near the wall, the working space will be gradually reduced until there's no more room for the blind nailer. Switch back to the face nailer and nail as you did on the first few courses, using the same schedule. The last few courses closest to the wall can be pried or "pulled" into place using a prybar against scraps of flooring to protect the wall or by using scraps of flooring as a lever and fulcrum, as shown in the photo below at left.

If you don't have a helper, sit on your butt and lever with your foot so both hands are free to operate the face nailer. Don't get too forceful with your prying, or you could puncture the drywall. The last piece (it's often quite narrow) will probably have to be ripped to width. It may also be necessary to remove the bottom portion of the groove so that it can be slipped in from above. I try to glue the last piece to the tongue of the previous piece. As shown in Figure 27 on p. 81, small wedges driven between the piece and the wall act as clamps.

A long flooring strip acts as a lever to pull the last course tight against its neighbor (below left). The strips on the wall act as a fulcrum and protect the drywall against damage. Counterbored screw holes are covered with wooden plugs (below right).

One way of avoiding the weak joint caused by ripping off the groove is to glue the last piece to the last full course before it's nailed down. When the glue has cured, fasten both at once with face nails. I keep a few strips of 3-in. plank handy when doing 2¼-in. flooring. Often, a 3-in. piece ripped to 2½ in. or 2¾ in. saves you having to cut and deal with a narrow rip.

To complete the floor, make or buy wooden plugs for the screw holes. Squirt some glue in the holes and tap the plugs home. When the glue has cured, use a sharp chisel to pare the projecting plugs flush with the surface of the flooring. Or wait until you're ready to sand the floor, at which time you can flush off the plugs with the edger.

I wait a minimum of one week and sometimes as long as a month or more before sanding a new floor. The wood needs time to acclimate to its new environment and to relax from the stress of being nailed and screwed to a flat surface. In very dry or very wet climates, wait at least a month. If you rush sanding, normal fractures that open up between boards can become exaggerated, requiring more sanding or filling. A floor that needs to be walked upon while it's acclimating can be protected against dirt and stains by a temporary cardboard or plywood cover.

Most unfinished flooring can stand up to even heavy foot traffic for considerable periods of time without a great deal of harm. The primary concern should be over spills such as water, solvents, sealers, lacquers, stains, paints, mortar and drywall compound.

Wooden plugs are pared flush with a chisel or left for the edging sander.

Notes on plank

Side-and-end-matched plank is installed like strip floor-ing, with a few differences. Layout and racking can be done as with strip; however, with plank, you often have the option of installing planks of variable width in the same floor. This can create a rustic look that many people like, especially in log homes, timber-frame homes or his-toric structures. A variable-width floor consists of specif-ic widths of plank repeating at regular row intervals. A random-width floor consists of random widths of plank in randomly appearing rows. A common variable-width floor is 3-in., 5-in. and 7-in. planks, in regular repeating rows.

When the planks are racked, of course, it's done by width for each course using an equal number of 3-in.,

5-in. and 7-in. rows to complete the floor. As with strip, planking should be perpendicular to the joists unless un-derlayment has been installed, as explained in Chapter 3. Indeed, underlayment is even more important with plank than with strip flooring, particularly with the wider boards. This is because a plank floor has fewer fasteners per square foot of coverage area than does strip, and the wider the boards, the more they tend to move with mois-ture changes.

Along with the movement comes squeaks, creaks and cupping—a common complaint with plank flooring. It's ironic that one of the prime uses of plank is in vacation homes. Such structures usually endure long periods with-out heat, then are abruptly heated up with dry wood heat. Such treatment results in extreme shifts in moisture con-

Side-and-end-matched plank flooring is blind nailed just like strip flooring. However, because of its width, plank flooring has fewer fasteners per square foot so it should also be face nailed or screwed.

tent. Fortunately, most vacation homes are expected to look rustic, so the inevitable cupping, crowning and gapping of boards are considered charming.

Driving additional blind nails to help secure planking does some good, but in flooring that is wider than 4 in., I recommend that planks also be face nailed or screwed to the subflooring or joists as well. For this I use 2-in. No. 12 square-drive flat-head wood screws. It's okay to use longer screws to penetrate well into the joists. I generally use square-drive screws, not because they are stronger but because they are very fast to drive with an electric screwgun. Unlike slotted screws or Phillips-head screws, square-drive screws almost never strip. Drywall screws are a very tempting substitute, but they have a tendency to snap off.

The jig shown above right marks screw holes for boring. Planks can be fastened to the joists with square-head wood screws (right) whose countersunk holes are plugged.

Plugs can accent a plank floor.

Even if the boards are end matched, but particularly if they are not, be sure to face nail or screw end butts into subflooring or joists. If you are lucky enough to have very long planks, face nail or screw portions of the field as well. Fastening at every other joist is a good interval. Plank can be face nailed with an air nailer or by hand. A number of nail types are effective, including decorative head nails sold expressly for this purpose or twist-shank flooring nails.

I plug the screw holes with wood plugs whose grain is turned perpendicular to that of the planks for a decorative effect. Besides, it's easier to hide the fact that you didn't want to spend time cutting plugs that would line up with the surrounding grain. Another common approach to covering the screw holes is to use plugs or dowels made from a contrasting wood species, as shown in the photo at left. Walnut is a nice touch.

Whether you use screws or nails, you should follow a pattern that looks appealing to you. If possible, avoid an unsightly line of fasteners close to the wall across the butt ends (Figure 28).

Figure 28 **Fastening Planks**

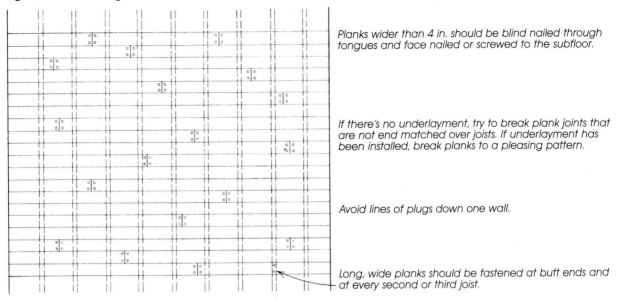

Planks wider than 4 in. should be blind nailed through tongues and face nailed or screwed to the subfloor.

If there's no underlayment, try to break plank joints that are not end matched over joists. If underlayment has been installed, break planks to a pleasing pattern.

Avoid lines of plugs down one wall.

Long, wide planks should be fastened at butt ends and at every second or third joist.

Installed tile by tile, even a Rhombus pattern parquet like the one above can usually be installed faster than a strip or plank floor, given the same area.

Parquet:
Layout and Installation

Chapter 5

W hen potential clients come to my shop in search of flooring, I'm always surprised at how quickly most of them rule out parquet. I'd say that fewer than one out of every 50 jobs I do is parquet. For clients wanting to contract a floor, a prime concern is cost; anything that looks as sumptuous as parquet has got to be ruinously expensive, especially when it comes near the end of the construction budget (as is usually the case with flooring).

Although it takes some persuasion, I'm usually able to explain that even some of the complicated parquet patterns are in fact easier (but not necessarily faster) to install than strip or plank, at least in a square or rectangular room without a lot of cut-up space. For simple patterns like Finger Block, I usually figure that a parquet floor requires about 25% less work during installation than the equivalent area in strip or plank.

Depending on the grade, species, thickness and pattern, parquet is often cheaper than strip or plank. That said, parquet might not be right for every room in the house. Like a rich dessert, a little of it goes a long way. Intricate patterns like diamond or herringbone may look attractive in a single room, but vast expanses of the stuff may be more than you can stand. Moreover, some parquet patterns are acutely direction sensitive, which means laying them one way will look fine but laying them another way will look just awful. The only way to find out for certain is to "dry lay" trial patterns on the subfloor and have a look.

The best way to find out how a parquet pattern will look is to dry lay a portion of it.

Parquet materials and design

Even though it's not as widely used as strip and plank, parquet flooring is sold in considerable variety. Well-stocked flooring suppliers are almost certain to have on hand popular patterns like $5/16$-in. thick Finger Block and Haddon Hall. Most suppliers should be able to order any pattern or species you want. As mentioned in Chapter 2, you can design your own parquet and have it made (for a price that may be breathtaking) by mills that specialize in custom work.

Parquet is sold in a multitude of sizes and thicknesses. The most common thicknesses are $5/16$ in. and $3/4$ in.; tile sizes vary greatly, depending on the pattern. The most common sizes in the thinner tiles are 11x11, 12x12, $13\frac{1}{4}$x$13\frac{1}{4}$ and 19x19. In thicker parquet, common square tile sizes are 9 in., $13\frac{1}{2}$ in., 18 in., and $22\frac{1}{2}$ in. Thicker parquet patterns are sometimes found in very large tiles, even up to 3 ft. or 4 ft.

Generally, the thinner the block, the more easily the pattern lends itself to glue-down installation. But most people find the larger, thicker strips and pieces easier to handle (especially when cutting) than the thinner material. This is one of the reasons that laminated products came into being. They're glued to a plywood-like structure and are easier to handle and more stable than solid parquet. Laminated parquet stays put better on most subfloors, regardless of the adhesive.

To hold them together during handling, the individual pieces that form parquet tiles are held together by a web backing, paper facing, or by a plastic or metal spline. Some are even edge glued. Web backing is the most common method for unfinished parquet in the thin, simple patterns. The webbing is porous to allow the adhesive to grab to the underside of the parquet when the tiles are set into the glue. Often four tiles are combined to form a single block; sometimes a block is composed of 16 or more tiles. The larger the block, the more unwieldy it is to handle, but the faster the installation will go.

With paper facing, the parquet is set with the paper facing up. Then, before the adhesive sets up, the paper is dampened with a sponge and removed. This is done before the glue sets completely so the tiles can still be moved to even out gaps. Soft metal or plastic splines are the usual binding agent for thick parquet. The splines are soft enough to be cut without damaging ordinary sawblades.

Preparation and layout

Because parquet is made up of small pieces running in different directions, don't count on a parquet floor adding any structural integrity to a subfloor. Most parquet requires adding an underlayment to your subfloor. Even on a slab, a $3/4$-in. underlayment can help cushion undulations in the concrete and act as a vapor barrier. It also softens the overall feel of the floor. But as long as there's no acute moisture problem, it's okay to glue parquet directly to a concrete slab.

If you try to lay parquet directly over an old hardwood floor, car decking or a plywood deck whose condition is questionable, you'll be in for big trouble. The tiles will never lie flat, and piece by piece, they'll work themselves loose. If you aren't willing to spare the expense and work of installing underlayment, do yourself a favor and use strip or plank flooring instead.

Underlayment should be a minimum of $1/2$-in. ACX plywood, nailed over the existing subfloor (see pp. 50-51), although $1\frac{1}{8}$ in. of plywood is ideal, if height gain isn't a problem. Always leave a gap of $1/8$ in. between underlayment sheets and along wall lines for expansion. This is particularly important with parquet. If sheets are placed too close together, expansion could cause their edges to lift, loosening the parquet's bond.

A concrete slab should be checked for level, flatness and moisture content, as described on pp. 46-50. Any contamination like paint, grease, oil or adhesive residue should be removed. Many slabs will have been sealed against moisture, but unless you're certain that the sealer is compatible with the adhesive you intend to use, remove the sealer as described on p. 49 and start over again with fresh sealer.

For the parquet floor illustrated in this chapter, I had to strip off a layer of carpet and the adhesive sticking the pad to the concrete. I couldn't tell if the slab had been sealed, so I sanded it with a floor sander, just to be sure. Mine was an old slab with no signs of migrating moisture. I took a risk in deciding not to reseal it. The adhesive I used is solvent based, and although it's not a true sealer, it will help keep moisture from migrating through the slab into the parquet.

As with strip and plank, design and layout should proceed from one or more focal points. The baseline method is the usual layout procedure but because the flooring is laid in a gridwork that involves going in two directions at once, two or more baselines (sometimes called working lines) are necessary, as shown in Figure 29.

Determining how layout affects focal points is trickier with parquet than with strip or plank. This is because the direction a parquet floor is laid has more impact on the way the room looks than does strip or plank, especially with patterns like Herringbone. A focal point can be any prominent feature in the room, and as with strip and plank, the parquet can be laid right up to a border.

In designing the floor, take special care to locate all of the major focal points and viewing points as well as any lesser areas whose prominence will set them apart from the visual busyness the pattern is likely to create. I've found the best way to do this is not by drawing the floor plan, but by actually dry laying the pattern with a dozen or more tiles in the middle of the floor. By orienting the tiles in different directions and viewing the results from var-

Figure 29 Parquet Layout

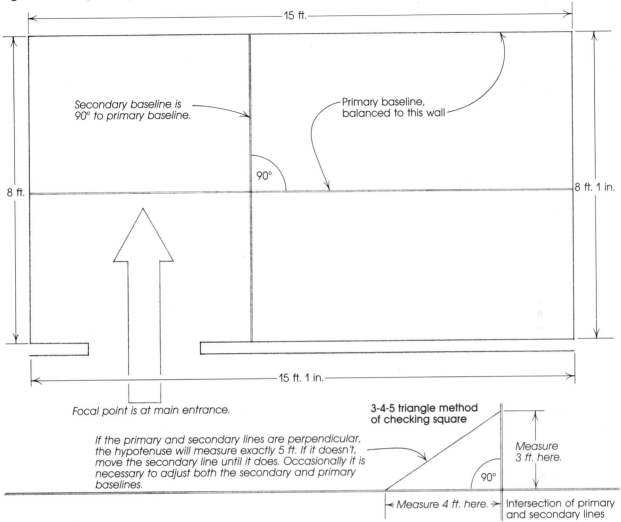

15 ft.

Secondary baseline is
90° to primary baseline.

Primary baseline,
balanced to this wall

90°

8 ft.

8 ft. 1 in.

15 ft. 1 in.

Focal point is at main entrance.

If the primary and secondary lines are perpendicular,
the hypotenuse will measure exactly 5 ft. If it doesn't,
move the secondary line until it does. Occasionally it is
necessary to adjust both the secondary and primary
baselines.

3-4-5 triangle method
of checking square

Measure
3 ft. here.

90°

Measure 4 ft. here.

Intersection of primary
and secondary lines

ious parts of the room, I get a good sense of what the finished floor will look like. As I'm viewing sample layouts, I try to visualize how the various patterns I'm trying will relate to the focal points. If I spot any problems, I'll try another arrangement to resolve them.

As I explained earlier in the book, parquet floors create a gridwork or pattern rather than advancing across the subfloor in a single direction, as strip does. Parquet is therefore laid in two directions at once, pyramid fashion, along an x-axis and a y-axis. This requires two intersecting baselines or working lines that are exactly perpendicular to each other. Both lines must be adjusted for any out-of-parallel or out-of-square the room happens to have.

Some floor mechanics strike these two lines so they intersect near the center of the room, then lay the tiles outward, into the corners. Others prefer to work out of one corner into the rest of the room, just as you would with

strip or plank. I like the center-out method in a hall or in a room with lots of details to cut around, such as cabinets or doorways. In an open square or rectangular room, the corner-out method is faster and usually works fine.

Begin by measuring the room for squareness and wall parallelism. I like to record the numbers on a rough sketch of the floor plan, as shown in Figure 29. Next, pick the focal points or, if none suggest themselves, pick a "primary wall," the one that will be most obvious upon entering the room. The primary wall will serve as the datum for one of the baselines and along this wall, you'll want the tiles to fit with no obvious tapers or runout. For illustration purposes, the room shown in Figure 29 is shaped like a trapezoid, with no parallel walls. This means that the primary-wall baseline will have to be balanced to hide the error, as explained on pp. 60-62 and in Figure 29.

Figure 30 **Tile Fall**

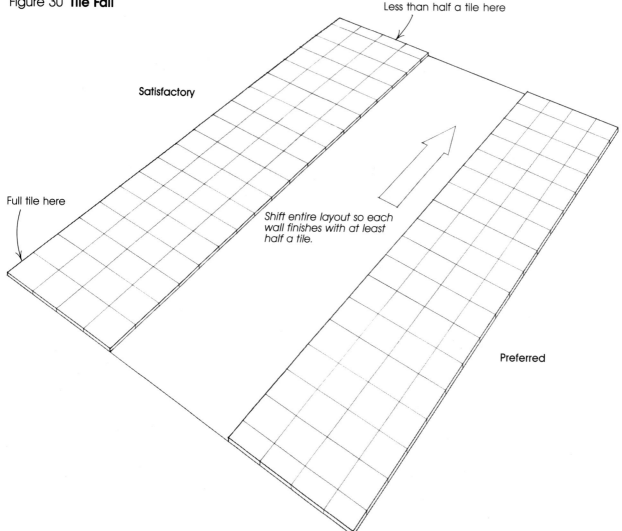

Less than half a tile here

Satisfactory

Full tile here

Shift entire layout so each wall finishes with at least half a tile.

Preferred

One big difference between strip or plank and parquet is that in placing the baselines for parquet, you have to account for tile "fall," the manner in which the individual tiles meet each wall. Ideally, the tiles would fall so you end up with exactly a full tile at every wall. In the real world, of course, this never happens. Try to locate the baselines so each wall butts to at least half the tile width (Figure 30).

Accounting for tile fall is easy when the tiles you're installing are square and the room you're installing them in has parallel walls. All you do is measure the room's dimensions, then center the baseline to achieve balanced tile fall. If, as is usually the case, you can't make the fall balance with half a tile or more to all wall lines, try to lay the tiles so the fractional pieces are in inconspicuous parts of the floor. The secondary line should also be struck with tile-fall considerations in mind. However, as

far as the secondary line goes, balanced tile fall is less important than having the secondary line absolutely perpendicular to the primary line.

If these two aren't perpendicular, you risk a nightmare runout as the tiles approach the secondary wall. The reason for having perpendicular lines is to keep the tile laying from getting out of whack. Never count on the tiles themselves to be square. Unfinished parquet is notorious for having sizes variances up to ⅛ in. or more. Sometimes you'll find you have tiles whose sizes vary slightly within the same box. Worse yet is to find regular-sized tiles in three or four boxes and begin to depend on it, only to get off-size tiles in the next four boxes.

To strike the secondary line, balance it as best you can, then check to be sure that it is perpendicular with the primary line. If you need to adjust the layout, reposition the secondary line, leaving the primary line where it is. In

For the floor in this narrow hallway, the installer establishes the primary baseline by centering it between the two long walls. Measure at several points along the wall, as shown below.

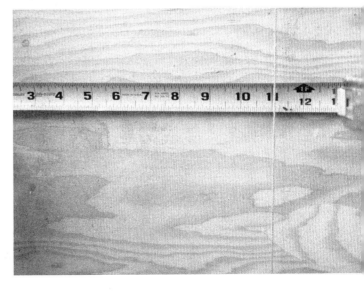

the worst cases, you'll need to adjust both lines to balance the alignment visually. I recommend using the 3-4-5 triangle method to do this (see Figure 29 on p. 91). First, find the center point on the primary baseline by measuring from both walls. Measure out 4 ft. along your primary baseline to the right or left of this axis and mark a point. Next, strike a mark 3 ft. up or down your proposed secondary baseline. The diagonal measurement from mark to mark should be 5 ft. If it isn't, adjust the secondary line.

Check the layout by dry laying several boxes of tiles. If your tiles are rectangular instead of square, as with Herringbone, you'll still need perpendicular baselines. Herringbone typically requires frequent if not continuous perpendicular baselines throughout the installation area to keep the tiles from running out of whack. Remember, when you balance either the primary or secondary baselines, to take into account any differences in the tiles' length and width.

As with strip and plank, parquet can be laid on the diagonal, creating a diamond pattern from what would otherwise be squares. Figure 31 shows the diagonal-layout method. With square tiles, using a center balanced layout, the tile fall will be automatically balanced.

Laying parquet

Before I explain laying tile, I should talk a bit about adhesives. The most common wood-flooring adhesives in use today can be grouped into one of three categories: cold-tar mastics or "cutback," water-based mastics, latex or emulsions, and chlorinated solvent mastics. Each of these has advantages and disadvantages, but as far as working

qualities go, you're looking for an adhesive to "flash" quickly, which means that it initially cures enough to become tacky. An adhesive's open working time—specified in minutes or hours—is a measure of how long the exposed surface will remain tacky enough to work with.

Cold-tar mastic or "cutback" is the traditional adhesive for parquet and other floors and is still widely used today, especially for ¾-in. parquet. It's inexpensive and is a good choice where a polyethylene film is required as a vapor barrier. It's also flammable, smelly and messy to use and clean up, and has a tendency to bleed up between pieces or through porous wood fibers. There's also some concern over the toxicity of the solvents used to thin the mastic, so be sure to wear a respirator and gloves. Let it flash off at least four to six hours before installing over it.

Figure 31 **Diagonal Layout**

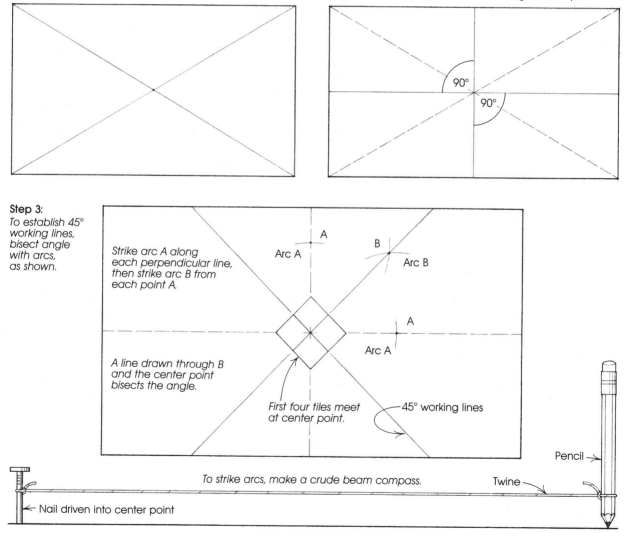

Step 1: *With diagonal lines, find room's center.*

Step 2: *Strike perpendicular lines through center point.*

90°
90°

Step 3:
To establish 45° working lines, bisect angle with arcs, as shown.

Strike arc A along each perpendicular line, then strike arc B from each point A.

A
Arc A
B
Arc B
A
Arc A

A line drawn through B and the center point bisects the angle.

First four tiles meet at center point.

45° working lines

To strike arcs, make a crude beam compass.

Pencil

Twine

Nail driven into center point

Parquet tiles are set with mastic-type adhesives. A few products claim to be both concrete sealer and adhesive. Most, however, require separate sealers when used over concrete.

I like the chlorinated solvent mastics best because they offer the most favorable combination of flash time, open working time, elasticity and longevity, even when exposed to excess moisture. They do require good ventilation and cleanup with a compatible solvent, usually paint thinner. If you happen to be using a chlorinated solvent over vinyl flooring, be sure you use a plasticizer-blocking sealer first, or the bond may be substantially weakened.

Water-based adhesives are by far the safest. They're nearly odorless, non-flammable and flash almost instantly. But, in my opinion, water-based adhesives aren't as durable as solvent-based adhesives, especially in moist conditions, such as you'd encounter over a concrete slab. One other type of adhesives, epoxy, is also occasionally used for flooring. Although it's moisture resistant, it's also messy and sets up too quickly into a brittle bond. This can cause a loose or noisy floor later on.

Whichever adhesive you pick, be sure to use the required protective equipment, especially an organic-vapor respirator with solvent and epoxy adhesives. Epoxy is a skin irritant for many people, so use thin plastic or rubber gloves when handling it. Always extinguish gas-range and water-heater pilot lights before spreading flammable adhesives or chlorinated solvent adhesives. Arrange the ventilation so that air near the floor, where vapors tend to settle, will be kept constantly moving.

The label on the adhesive can should give specifics on how to apply the material. It should also tell what size and type of trowel to use. I spread the solvent-based adhesive shown in the photos here with a $5/32$-in. V-notch trowel. A notched trowel is more effective than a flat one because the notches automatically meter the amount of adhesive being applied and the proper ridge depth. If you spread too much, the tiles won't seat flat and the excess adhesive will ooze up between the joints, a real mess that will take forever to dry. Too little adhesive creates an inferior bond, resulting in loose tiles, another real mess since it's not easy to reset a tile later.

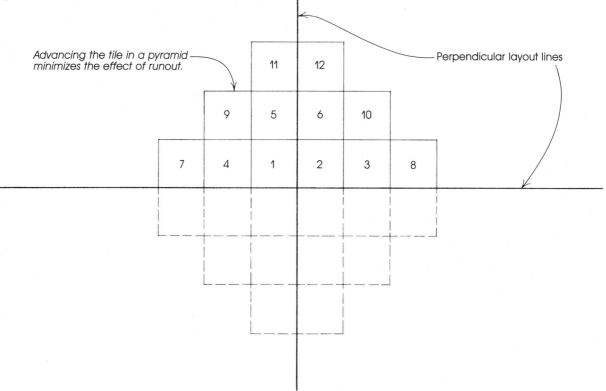

Figure 32 **Pyramid Layout**

Advancing the tile in a pyramid minimizes the effect of runout.

Perpendicular layout lines

Begin laying by opening and unpacking a couple of boxes of tiles. Stack these nearby, within easy reach of where you'll be working. In the photos on the facing page, I was tiling a small hallway, so I started at one end and moved down the center of the hall, working out toward the walls. In an open room, I start in the center, at the intersection of the two layout lines, and work into the corners, as shown in Figure 32.

Spread an even layer of adhesive, as shown in the top photos on the facing page. Depending on the adhesive's open time (which varies with the product and the temperature), I coat several square feet at a time. Just pick up a generous dollop of adhesive on the corner of the trowel and work it across the surface in a sweeping, semicircular motion. As you cover more area, try to work your sweeps from the dry area into the wet area.

When you've covered a big enough working area, let the adhesive flash. Usually, this occurs in a few minutes. You can test for tackiness with your finger. If it has flashed, the adhesive will feel tacky or soft and slightly rubbery. In any case, be sure the mastic remains "wet" or sticky until you've had a chance to mount the tiles or strips into it. If not, you'll have to scrape up the dry material and apply fresh. Trowel adhesive immediately adjacent to and away from your baselines. It's usually possible to see the layout lines through the adhesive, but if

the coat is thick, the lines may be obscured. Some floor mechanics rechalk the layout lines on top of the adhesive layer, once it has flashed. This is a good idea, at least for the first few courses, which should be positioned as accurately as possible.

Position the first tile so its edges line up with both baselines, as shown in the bottom photo on the facing page. The adhesive should be pliable enough to allow the tile to be moved back and forth a bit to achieve perfect alignment with the working lines. Once it's positioned where you want it, "seat" the tile by pushing down firmly with your hands, starting at the center and working out toward the edges. Another way of seating the tile is to tap it with a hammer. Protect the tile's surface against marring with a scrap wooden block, or use a rubber mallet.

If the adhesive is not pliable and does not immediately "grab" the parquet when you set it, the adhesive has set and will not hold properly. Remove the dry adhesive and apply fresh material. Continue laying tiles following the pyramid pattern shown in Figure 32. Why not lay in rows? Because the tiles are rarely square, nor are they of uniform size. In fact, from box to box and lot to lot, errors of as much as $\frac{1}{8}$ in. are not uncommon. If you lay in rows, these errors, no matter how slight, will accumulate into one gigantic mess. The pyramid approach allows you to build the pattern accurately out from the center.

With a generous dollop on a notched trowel (left), spread the adhesive in sweeping arcs (above), or pour a blob on the floor and spread with a trowel. Work the adhesive away from fixed objects like walls and headers. Using the baseline as a reference, set each tile and bed it firmly in the adhesive, as shown below.

Each new row is referenced to at least one accurate line, so errors don't have much chance to accumulate. Those that do can be corrected by fudging the position of whatever tile happens to be causing the problem, or by adjusting the tiles to either side of it. This technique results in some gaps between tiles but with unfinished tiles, these can be averaged out as you lay the tiles, then filled during sanding later on.

As the floor field enlarges from the center, you may wish to work atop plywood sections or squares and place others down on traffic paths over recently installed areas. Until the adhesive cures, the tiles are tender and will move out of alignment if you step on them at the wrong

angle. Plywood can also help keep a prefinished floor from getting too dirty. Once installation is complete, however, remove the plywood so that the floor can get maximum ventilation and solvents contained in the adhesive will readily evaporate through the floor's surface.

Work the tiles out from the center, toward the walls. As you approach the wall, mark and cut full tiles into the pieces necessary to abut the wall. Rather than measuring, I hold the full tile in place then scribe it with a pencil, as shown in the top photo on the facing page. Make sure to position the trimmed tile correctly so the partial pattern it represents matches the full pattern on the adjacent tile. For the Finger Block tile I used here, maintaining the pat-

Minor gaps between parquet tiles are unavoidable. Even them out by moving the tiles horizontally, then plan to fill the gaps during sanding. With prefinished flooring, fill after the installation is completed and the adhesive is fully cured.

tern was relatively easy. With more complex designs, it may be more difficult to get an exact match.

Cutting parquet tiles can be an ordeal. Whether the tile is bound by cloth webbing, paper facing or metal spline, the individual pieces always seem to want to go their separate ways. The ideal tool for cutting parquet is a bandsaw with a thin, fine-tooth blade. A bandsaw cuts cleanly and with minimum vibration so the pieces tend to remain attached to the binding. An acceptable alternative is a hand jigsaw or, in a pinch, a scrollsaw. I don't recommend a using table saw or radial-arm saw, because the vibration of these tools will tend to pop pieces loose, possibly causing a jam or violent kickback.

Position tiles to be trimmed for marking (right), then saw them to size with the bandsaw or with a scrollsaw (below).

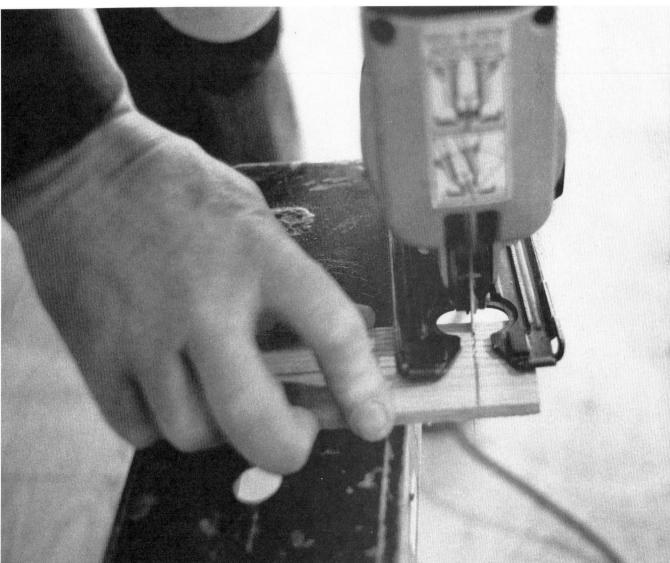

I trim the tiles outside of my pencil lines with unfinished tiles so I'll be sure to have a tight fit. Before you set the trimmed tile, check once more to see that its pattern matches the next full tile. Once you have set the pieces you cut, you will have a sticky mess to contend with around your saws or tools. Slip the trimmed tile into place, and then seat it with gentle hammer taps.

Because the grain in parquet tiles runs in many different directions, the effects of wood movement should be somewhat self-canceling. All the same, I like to leave an expansion gap at the walls, if only to make cutting and fitting less bothersome. The gap will be covered by the baseboard. As you can see in the photo at right on the facing page, parquet is simply butted to headers and borders. A lot of prefinished parquet and thicker tiles are tongue-and-groove, and these should be mated to headers and borders just as strip or plank flooring would be (see pp. 76-77).

If you're laying parquet over plywood underlayment, you have the option of face nailing it here and there, say where a balky tile just won't lie flat or where a header may have warped a bit. Use a 4d or 6d finish nail and set it well below the surface. Once the main part of the floor is tiled and the walls trimmed, you may want to set the parquet by rolling it with a 150-lb. roller. Floor mechanics who do lots of glue-down work have special rollers for this purpose, but if you don't have one and can't rent one,

an ordinary lawn roller will do. Just make sure that the roller is clean and dry.

You can also use a rubber mallet to "set" each tile individually before going on. Note that some products should not be rolled. Check the cartons or installation instructions for the parquet you're using. If you do roll the floor, check the tiles for gaps. At this point, the adhesive should be soft enough so that you can correct the most obvious gaps by carefully repositioning the individual tiles. Move the tiles by pushing them sideways with your shoe, fingers or a tool with a thin blade (like a putty knife or utility knife). Try to split the difference so one large gap becomes two smaller, more easily fillable gaps.

Glued-down parquet pieces can be fragile; they can easily be separated from their berths in exposed regions such as doorways and other transition areas. Borders, headers and reducers are more than ornaments in a good parquet installation; they also serve to protect the relatively delicate tile edges. It's a good idea to nail these pieces not only to hold the strips in place while the adhesive dries but also to secure them over the long haul, helping them absorb the brunt of wheeled or heavy foot traffic.

It sometimes becomes necessary to cut apart the individual slats in a tile to even out gaps. This can be done with the tile in place by running a utility-knife blade sharply down between the slats to sever the binding. Then move the pieces in the direction you need to even out the gaps.

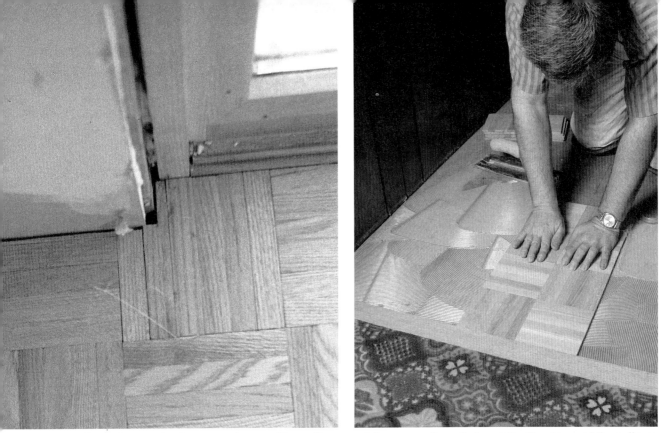

Although wood expansion is not a serious problem with parquet, leave a small gap between the tile edges and the walls, as shown at left. Where parquet butts to a border (right), install it as you would strip or plank flooring.

A wide, natural-bristle brush makes quick work of finishing the floor.

Sanding and Finishing

Chapter 6

When hardwood flooring fell out of fashion during the late 1960s, many of the trade's experienced hands retired or went on to other pursuits. The craft didn't quite become extinct, but during the late-1970s flooring resurgence, it became next to impossible to find a competent mechanic to sand and finish a floor. And with good reason. Sanding (and, to a lesser extent, finishing) is without a doubt the most demanding part of installing a hardwood floor. It's back-breaking, dusty work. To do it well (and quickly) requires a deft touch that comes with years of experience.

You may think I'm suggesting that you hire a professional to sand and finish the floor that you've so carefully installed. Although that's surely an option, I've found over the years that a dedicated do-it-yourselfer can achieve acceptable (if not respectable) results by substituting patience and a go-slow attitude for the floorman's years of experience. Because so many home owners have chosen to tackle the job themselves, there's a vigorous rental market for floor-sanding equipment and materials, along with some good technical advice when you run into problems.

In this chapter, I'll explain in detail how to prepare, sand, stain and finish a hardwood floor. Although I'm assuming you'll be dealing with a new hardwood floor, there's also information on refinishing an old floor. For floors I install, I recommend Swedish finish, a clear coating that's beautiful and durable. By customer request, I will also occasionally use oil-modified urethane (or polyurethane, as it's called in the wood-flooring trade), waterborne urethane, oil or just plain sealer and wax. The pros and cons of each are discussed briefly in the section on selecting a finish (see pp. 121-124).

Preparation

There's only one way to describe sanding and finishing a hardwood floor: it's a big mess. Get ready for lots of noise, dust and odor. Rooms being sanded will fill with a fine, choking dust. Even though you'll be masking off adjacent areas, dust will get everywhere, so you might as well resign yourself to a major cleanup job. You can make things easier by removing books, drapes, clothing and knickknacks from both the room to be sanded and rooms immediately adjacent. To seal doors, tape them with masking tape or duct tape (on the woodwork, not on the drywall), or tack old sheets or blankets over the door trim and seal the bottom of each door with a rolled-up towel wrapped with tape.

To seal adjacent rooms against dust, tape blankets over the doors and place rolled-up towels at the thresholds.

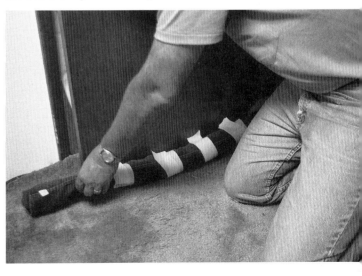

Before sanding, check the floor carefully for protruding nails. Set any you find well beneath the floor's surface.

A better way to fasten blankets over doors is with small nails or thumbtacks. Push pins work equally well with plastic or cloth for attaching to drywall. The holes they leave are usually less conspicuous than chipped paint and ripped drywall. Also, a blanket's weight will seal without being tacked around its entire perimeter, so you can lift a corner to pass through the door. When the job is done, a washing will reclaim the blanket.

Kitchen cabinets can also be sealed with tape. Vibration and dust-sensitive objects—stereo equipment, televisions, computers—should be moved as far from the sanding site as practical and covered with plastic or drop cloths, or moved to another building altogether. Breakable objects that might be vibrated off a shelf should be removed and stored safely.

Once sanding is done, plan on closing all windows, doors or any other openings that could permit moisture or drafts to contact the floor before the finish cures. Drafts (such as under an exterior door) will cause some finishes to blister, resulting in a rough final coat. If there's a mail slot in the front door, tape it shut. I remember one job where I forgot to do that and found the front page of the weekend newspaper glued to a freshly dried coat of Swedish finish.

During filling, staining and finishing, extinguish any open flames in the immediate area. Some of these compounds are highly flammable. It's usually not necessary to shut off pilot lights in furnaces, water heaters and gas ranges unless the work is to take place in the same room as these appliances.

One often overlooked item is electric power. When you installed the floor, there were probably plenty of 110-volt outlets for your chopsaw and drills. But are they up to powering a floor sander? Sanders require at least 20-amp circuits for 110-volt machines. Check the fuse or breaker box. In older houses, 15-amp circuits are common. How about 220-volt outlets for the bigger sanders? These should be at least 30 amp and accessible to the sander's long cord. Outlets for clothes dryers and ranges are usually adequate, but make sure the outlet's female pattern matches the male prongs on the sander. If the outlet is too far from the action, rent a heavy-duty extension cord from the sander supplier.

Make advance arrangements to keep all foot traffic off the floor during the entire sanding and finishing process. This may involve tacking doors shut, posting detour signs and even opening a window for temporary access. Traffic of any sort in the immediate or adjacent areas—pounding on walls outside or upstairs, for instance—will dislodge dust or debris onto the clean sanded floor or into the tacky finish.

When you installed the floor, you should have set all of the face nails at least ⅛ in. beneath the surface. Did you forget any? Now's the time to check. Walk the floor in a systematic way in areas where face nailing was necessary in a side-and-end-matched floor—mainly near the walls, at any unavoidable weak lines and so on. Reset any nails that don't look deep enough. I can't overemphasize the importance of setting nails. If the sander encounters a protruding nail, it'll make an expensive mess of the sandpaper and drum.

Flooring that's entirely face nailed—square-edge strip, plank or older parquet, will have to be checked carefully for set nails. Even so, nails have a habit of pushing their way back to the surface during sanding. Expect up to 5% of the nails to be "shiners" (nail heads flush with the surface) in such floors. You can reset them, if you like, between coats or after the job is complete, with finish putty.

Filling. Almost every new floor will need some filling to disguise the nail holes and seal obvious cracks. I usually use commercial fillers made expressly for the purpose. These products are described in detail on pp. 118-119. When to fill is a matter of personal preference. Some mechanics like to set the nails, spot fill the holes and sand, then refill the entire floor and sand again. Others like to

For floor sanding, you'll need at least one drum sander, an edger (spinner) and an assortment of sanding belts or sheets and discs. A heavy-duty shop vacuum is useful for cleaning up the dust.

sand first, then fill everything, and then sand again. That's the way I usually do it.

It doesn't really matter much, so long as you end up with a smooth floor that's filled where it needs to be. There are limits on what can be filled. Certainly nail holes and cracks between strips or holes within the individual strips should be filled on most new square-edge floors. If you installed the flooring correctly, there shouldn't be any large cracks or gaps. On old floors, however, years of seasonal movement and wear and tear will have opened up larger cracks. Gaps ⅛ in. or wider or shallow depressions in the flooring almost always refuse to hold filling compounds. Loose pieces or flooring that deflect with foot traffic will spit out filler very quickly, leaving sharp-edged, ugly protrusions of filler. Similarly, I don't recommend filling fir, pine, hemlock or other softwood floors that tend to "work" a lot with moisture changes. You are better off accepting the gaps as character.

Tools

Sanding and finishing a floor require very few tools (far fewer, in fact, than required to install it). But the most important of these—the sanding and buffing machines—are indispensable and are so specialized (and expensive) that renting them is the only practical option. Most rental stores and many wood-flooring dealers rent three kinds of machines: the drum sander, edge sander and buffer. On the typical job, all three will be needed at some point, although the resourceful owner-builder might be able to substitute hand scraping or a small belt sander (and some elbow grease) for the edger; and on small jobs, hand sanding will do in lieu of screening with a buffer.

The drum sander does the bull work, leveling the broad expanse of the floor, removing any old stain or finish and flattening any overwood. In areas the drum sander can't reach, such as close to the walls, the edger's rotating disc

Drum sanders are made in two styles, sheet fed (left) and belt (facing page).

will usually do the job. The buffer is used to blend the freshly sanded raw floor before staining and finishing. It's also used between coats of finish to remove raised grain and rough up a dried finish coat to prepare it for another coat. On waxed floors, the buffer is used to remove old wax and buff the new to a high shine. Technically, the buffer is not a sander, but as you'll see, it can be fitted with an abrasive screen capable of mild scouring of the floor surface. Most of what the buffer does can also be done with hand sanding.

Because these machines are expensive ($6,500 for a drum sander) you wouldn't expect them to rent cheaply. To keep from wasting money on an idle machine that you don't need, plan your work carefully. If you need a drum sander to level a rough subfloor, prepare the floor for sanding, rent the machine for half a day and return it. When it's time to finish sand the floor, rent both a drum sander and an edger and try to sand the entire job in one day. After the first coat of finish is applied, you can then rent the buffer.

The drum sander. The "big machine," the drum sander, removes medium amounts of wood or an old stain and finish by means of sandpaper wrapped around a rotating drum. The drum, made of metal, is sleeved with rubber to cushion contact with the floor and provide traction for the sandpaper. Drum sanders are specified by drum size (width), voltage, drum-elevating method and sandpaper type (sheet versus belt). Most sanders are made in 8-in., 10-in. or 12-in. widths. The most common size available at rental yards is 8 in., probably because it's lightest and is therefore easiest to handle. Also, most 8-in. sanders run on 110-volt power, a real convenience for do-it-yourselfers.

it should come as no surprise that sanding a floor will take longer with an 8-in. machine than with 10-in. or 12-in models. An 8-in. machine wired for 110 volts seems to run slower and have less power. On the plus side, the smaller machine is lighter and can be operated in tight quarters. This means less edger and hand work. Many professionals who do a lot of residential work and have to drag their tools up flights of stairs swear by the 8-in. ma-

Sanding belts are easier to install, but they cost a little more than sheets.

chines, although most prefer the more powerful 220-volt models. I highly recommend 110-volt drum sanders for the first-time user. Besides being easier to maneuver, the 8-in. machine's slower cutting rate will lessen the severity of the inevitable errors.

Most rental shops offer sanders that load paper in one of two ways, continuous belt or individual sheet. The belt models have less of a tendency to leave chatter marks and are generally easier to load than sheet-fed sanders. Belt tension is normally adjusted with a lever near the drive mechanism. Loosening the tension allows the belt to be slipped on and off. A separate tensioning device controls belt tracking, shifting the angle of the drum to move the belt from side to side. If you've ever used a belt sander, the principle is the same.

Sheet-fed drum sanders are much easier to find, less temperamental and less expensive to rent, but loading paper takes some practice. There are several common paper-loading designs. Some have a slot in the drum into which one end of a single sheet of paper is inserted. The slot is

on the bias relative to the drum's length, to minimize chatter marks and tearing of the paper. Once one end is inserted, the paper is wrapped around the drum and the other end is inserted in the same slot. Both ends are pulled inward and held tight by cams inside the slot that are activated by bolts on the ends of the drum. Another type locks the paper under a metal strip screwed to the drum. All of these are demonstrated on the videotape.

Sheet-fed machines can be frustrating to load. Getting the paper aligned with the drum and tight around its circumference takes some work and a certain knack that comes only from practice. A common mistake is not tucking the paper well enough into the slot before tightening down the cams. In order to get the finer grits of paper to hold tight on some machines, it's often necessary to insert a paper shim into the slot between the two ends of the paper before tightening down the cams.

Paper costs vary by machine type. Belts are more expensive than sheets, and coarse-grit paper is more expensive than fine-grit paper.

The drum sander at left is lowered into contact with the floor by tilting the entire machine.

To sand a floor, the operator moves the sander back and forth (with the grain, unless extra flattening is required or you are sanding parquet), removing material on both the forward and backward sweep. As this is done, the drum is lowered onto the floor at the beginning of each pass, then raised at the end. This raising and lowering of the drum feathers the start and stop of the individual passes, making for a smoother floor. The machine must be moving when the drum touches the floor; otherwise, a stop mark or cavity that is roughly the shape of the drum will be left in the floor surface.

There are two ways to raise and lower the drum: tilting the machine onto the floor by raising or lowering the handles, or manipulating a lever. The tilt design is by far the more common on rental machines. Tilt-drum machines are easier to use, less expensive to rent and have fewer parts to break. Most professionals prefer the lever-activated drum design. On this design, the drum is raised and lowered by means of a lever usually located just to the right of the handles. When adjusted correctly and used proper-

ly, lever machines do give a smoother feather than a tilt design. Unfortunately, keeping them adjusted is not easy, so I recommend the tilt design for infrequent users.

On some sanders, the position of the drum relative to the floor can be adjusted. This adjustment is usually made by turning a screw or moving a lever that raises or lowers one of the two primary wheels on which most of the sander's weight rests. Adjusting will cause the machine to cut deeper on either the left or right or evenly across the drum. If the machine you rent can be adjusted, ask the dealer to show you how it's done.

Every floor sander has his or her own way of adjusting the machine. Most set it to sand deeper on the left. With such a setting, the machine will feather best on the right side, and the machine should be worked across the room moving in rows that go from the right side of the room to the left. Floor mechanics who work in the opposite direction adjust the machine to sand deeper on the right. You can also adjust the drum for an even cut, which is not a bad idea for a beginner since a drum set for a flat cut will

This drum sander is lowered by a lever in the handle that operates a mechanism that pivots the drum.

remove far less material in a single pass. More and more, it seems, sanders manufactured for the rental market are designed according to the lowest-common-denominator theory: they're permanently set for a flat cut only.

As you might expect, rental rates for floor-sanding equipment vary considerably. In towns where few rental machines are available, expect to pay more than where there's lots of competition. Rental agencies often have combo packages (edger and drum sander and sometimes a buffer also) at a reduced cost over individual rental rates. Some have reduced weekend and holiday rates, others charge a premium for weekends. I've seen combo rates as low as $40 and as high as $150. Shop around and ask the rental agencies a few questions so you can develop a sense of how much help and advice they're willing to provide. Check with wood-flooring dealers or contractors first. They're more likely to have good machines and to provide you with useful expertise.

If you've never used a floor sander before (or even if you have), you'll need to observe some basic safety rules.

The machine is not inherently dangerous, but it can make a horrible mess if it gets away from you or if you accidentally get a finger or hand near the revolving drum. Always unplug the sander when you change the paper or adjust the machine. Don't attempt to adjust the machine with the motor running. Heavy drum sanders are equipped with belts that tie the handles to the operator. Use them. It will take most of the burden off your hands, arms and shoulders, and give the machine a smoother cut.

Sanders make an incredible racket. I always wear ear protectors of some kind. If I know I'll be doing a long day of sanding, I'll insert foam earplugs and put the hearing protectors over those. Lung and eye protection are critical too. Wear a nuisance-dust mask and eye protection of some kind to guard against flying dust and abrasive particles. If you are removing paint from a floor, have it tested for lead content first. You might prefer using a chemical stripper to sanding a lead-based paint. Similarly, some vinyl sheet goods and mastics contain asbestos. Have them tested before sanding or removing them.

Although both the big machine and the edger have dust-pickup systems built into them, don't expect all the fine dust to accumulate there. Large amounts of it will end up scooting out from under the machines or be blown out through the fibers of the bag. There are no dead man's switches on any floor machines that I know of except the buffers. So keep your hands on a running machine at all times, and memorize the position of the on/off switch.

The edger. Use the edger (spinner) where the big machine won't fit—close to the walls, closets and tight areas. There are several types of edgers. Most consist of a large motor connected directly to a shrouded disc 5 in. to 7 in. in diameter. The shroud has two wheels onto which most

of the machine's weight is directed. Each wheel is adjustable to vary the depth and angle of cut. A sandpaper disc is attached to the spinner plate, a rubber-faced disc set at a slight angle to the floor.

For its size, the edger removes more material per square foot than any other floor machine. It can be set to cut on the right or left near the center of the leading edge of the paper. Most pros like to "rough" a floor with the edger set slightly to the right of center with a fairly narrow cut, then widen or expand the cut to flatten it out as they get to finer and finer grits. If you're not careful, it's pretty easy to leave some nasty gouges. Fortunately, you'll get a lot of practice by rough and medium sanding before you have to do the final fine sanding. Another less common

Edge sanders have discs mounted on a single arbor (facing page). To widen the disc's footprint for feathering the cut, several discs can be mounted at once. An offset edger (right) can sand in restricted areas.

type of edger consists of a small (4-in. to 5-in. dia.) disc offset 1 ft. or more from the motor by a belt-and-pulley arrangement. The offset edger, which is shown in the photo above and in the videotape, allows you to reach up under obstructions, such as a cabinet toe space.

Ordinary power belt sanders and orbital vibrator hand sanders are really not designed for floor work. Except for tight spots and vertical areas, these tools are maddeningly slow and leave more sander marks than floor machines do. Recently, some manufacturers have introduced floor-style orbital vibrator machines. These are designed primarily to reduce hand sanding along edges and in corners. Some mechanics use them in place of screening with a buffer to blend various parts of the floor together.

Buffer. Although you can get by without one, for a really nice finish I recommend that you rent a buffer. This piece of equipment used to be indispensable during the heyday of waxed floors. Nowadays the buffer comes in handy for a final, fine abrading of the floor before staining or finishing to help blend all the areas of the floor together. Most buffers can be fitted with a screenback, a fine abrasive disc that looks something a like an insect screen coated with abrasive particles. Screens come in various diameters to fit buffers and in grits from 60 grit to 180 grit.

Screening between coats of finish will "take the tops off" (flatten raised grain), making for a smoother final finish. It will also provide "tooth" so the next coat of finish will adhere better. Ask your dealer about providing the

Although not absolutely necessary, a buffer with a screen-back is useful for final sanding and for smoothing raised grain between coats of finish.

buffer with screenbacks in various grits, a pad pusher and a buffing pad. A pad pusher is nothing more than a disc-shaped adapter, often wood, that allows the screenback to be driven by the buffer. One type is shown in the video-tape. Use the buffing pad as a cushion between the pad pusher and the screenback. If a screenback is not available, a medium-grit buffing pad will usually work as well to take the tops off and smooth raised grain.

Very rarely will you find a buffer with a dust-collection system. However, buffers do make dust. The dust from the final screening before staining or finishing is particularly fine and pervasive. It's good stuff to mix with a lacquer base to make filler.

Sandpaper. Sandpaper for floor machines is generally available in a range from 12 grit to 150 grit (the higher the number, the finer the grit and therefore the smoother the surface). For reference, I classify 12 grit to 20 grit as open-coat papers, 24 grit to 40 grit as rough, 50 grit to 80 grit as medium, and anything above 80 grit as fine. Most of these grits are commonly available in both sheet and belt form with paper or cloth as the backing material.

The harshest, most aggressive papers (12 grit, 16 grit and 20 grit) are open coat, which means that the abrasive particles are glued to the backing paper (or cloth) in such a way that open spaces between particles keep the paper from clogging and quickly becoming useless when sanding resinous woods or when removing a painted or thick waxes. Whenever possible, avoid using open-coat sand-paper. Although it cuts fast, it leaves deep scratches that require several separate sandings with progressively finer paper to remove. Use open-coat paper only as a last resort. The finer papers are closed coat, meaning that the abrasive particles cover 100% of the backing material. By dint of their finer grits, closed-coat papers don't last as long and tend to clog in resinous woods.

Five classes of abrasives are used on sandpapers. Three of them—flint, garnet and emery—are natural minerals; two—aluminum oxide and silicon carbide—are manmade. For general floor-sanding work, I prefer silicon carbide for rough sanding because it cuts very aggressively and holds up well. For fine work, I like garnet paper. It heats up less than the other abrasives and, in my opinion, does a better job. It's also reasonably priced.

For most new floor work (except parquet), you shouldn't need paper any coarser than 36 grit or finer than 120 grit. If you're sanding an old floor, you may want to start with a 16-grit or 20-grit open-coat paper, especially if the floor is coated with paint, a thick layer of varnish or wax. Most new floors will require a three-paper process, starting with 36 grit or 50 grit for roughing, 60 grit or 80 grit for medium sanding and 100 grit or 120 grit for finishing. You can sand finer, of course, if you're willing to spend the time and money. I suggest buying the paper from the shop where you rent the sander. Most shops will let you return what you don't use, so buy plenty.

Rough sanding

Whether you're sanding a new floor or an old one, the basics are pretty much the same. You'll start with coarse grits and proceed to finer grits, finally ending up with a 100-grit or 120-grit screen on the buffer. Somewhere during this sanding, the floor will be filled and resanded. The first task is to get the floor flat and all the old stain and finish removed, if it's an old floor. A new floor will almost always have some overwood (variations in height between adjacent strips). The amount of overwood depends on the subfloor, the underlayment and the accuracy of the milling process in the first place.

Unless the floor is painted, loaded with old finish or in really bad shape, I usually start with 36-grit paper, preferably a silicon carbide. If there's not much overwood or old finish to remove, I'll use a 50-grit or 60-grit paper to start. If it doesn't clog up quickly, you're better off starting with a finer grit for roughing. If you're a novice, start in an inconspicuous spot in a back room. That way, any errors won't be as noticeable. If you're sanding only one or two rooms, start at mid-room, where there will be a rug.

Before you actually begin with the drum sander, however, flush off any screw plugs with the edger or with a sharp chisel and set any visible nails you may have missed, As shown in Figure 33, begin near the right wall at a point a third of the way down the floor. (I am assuming here that the sander has been adjusted to cut slightly deeper on the left side of the drum, as explained in the drum-sander section. If the sander cuts deeper on the right, start on the opposite wall.) Start the sander and, while pushing it forward, slowly lower the rotating drum onto the floor. It's essential that the sander be moving when the drum engages the floor, or you'll have a hard-to-remove dip.

Figure 33 **Sanding Direction**

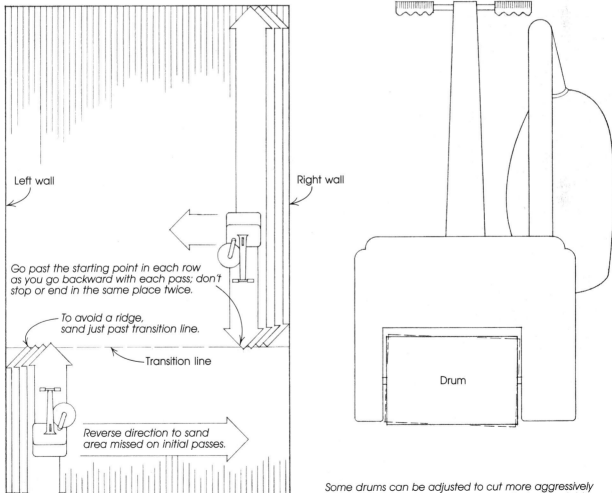

Left wall

Right wall

Go past the starting point in each row as you go backward with each pass; don't stop or end in the same place twice.

To avoid a ridge, sand just past transition line.

Transition line

Reverse direction to sand area missed on initial passes.

Drum

Some drums can be adjusted to cut more aggressively on the left or right side. For a drum adjusted for right-hand cutting, start sanding on the right wall, as shown.

To keep the sander's cord out of harm's way, hang it on a belt clip fashioned from a coat hanger (above) or drape it over your shoulders (left).

As the drum comes into contact with the floor, the weight of the sander will do all the work. The drum will pull the machine along so you'll have to regulate the speed to a slow shuffle, about 1 ft. to 2 ft. per second. Normal steps will cause you to tilt the machine from side to side, so take slow, deliberate steps, as if you are dancing with the sander. Watch out for the cord! I don't know how many rental machines I've gotten back with cords that have been run over and chewed up by the drum. It doesn't do the drum any good either. I wrap the cord around my shoulders and keep an eye on it at all times. If

you're not used to running a big sander, it really helps to have an assistant hold the cord to keep it out of your path. For the edger and buffer cords, I use a cord clip made from a coat hanger, shown in the photo above right.

Continue sanding until you're about 1 ft. from the wall, then lift the drum and lower it again as you pull the sander back in the opposite direction over the same path. Keep your arms extended but bent at the elbows and lean slightly backward as you draw it with you. Sand just past your starting point, then lift the drum gradually and repeat this process. This time, however, you will shift the sander

2 in. to 4 in. to the left. Continue in this manner until you reach the left wall. Then reverse direction and sand the area that you skipped when starting the first passes. Always sand a few feet past the transition point where you stopped when you sanded the other end of the room. This will help feather any slight ridges that might have been created where you changed directions.

Figure 33 on p. 113 shows a dream-world floor, all nice and open and rectangular. Figure 34, which shows my living room and dining room, is more like the real world. It's broken up by a partition wall, and the flooring runs in a direction that's far from ideal. For this floor, I broke the plan into two areas separated by a transition line, as shown in Figure 34. I then sanded both sides of the transition line, feathering the line.

On really uneven floors or on old floors, you may have to flatten the surface and remove old stain and finish by sanding at 45°, as shown in Figure 35. You'll probably have to start with 36-grit paper. Begin in one corner. Sand about two-thirds of the area, reverse direction and com-

Figure 35 **Diagonal Sanding**

Start in the left or right corner, depending on how the drum is adjusted. Reverse direction after sanding two-thirds of the floor.

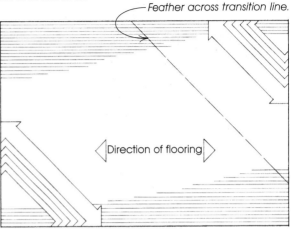

When the floor is flat, sand with the grain with the roughest grit to remove crossgrain scratching.

Figure 34 **Sanding an Irregular Room**

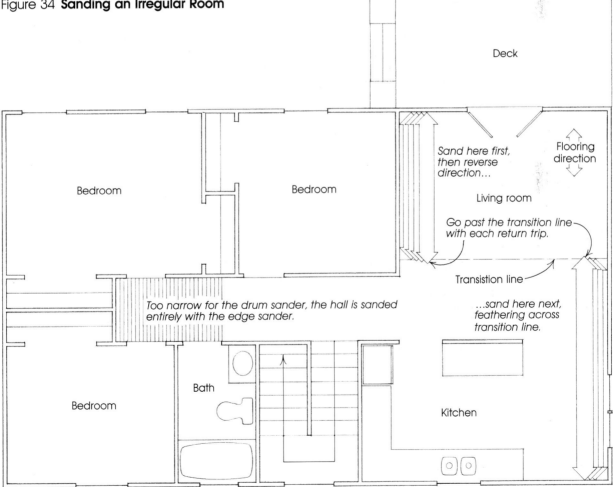

Stopping the sander while it's running will result in drum marks (left). Deep ones will have to be removed by sanding the damaged area diagonally (above).

plete the job. When the floor is mostly clean and flat, begin sanding with the grain with the same grit paper used for diagonal sanding. Don't try to remove diagonal scratches with your next grit paper. It won't work.

The two big errors you can make with the drum sander are drum marks and ridges. Drum marks happen when you lift or lower the drum too quickly or stop with the drum in contact with the floor. Really bad drum marks can't be removed without noticeable dipping. You may have to sand on the diagonal to clean them up (see the photos above). Ridges happen when you sand across the same spot in the floor several times without moving the sander over to feather your pass. Ridges at midfloor can be removed the same as drum marks. Those near the wall line must be taken out with the edger. Chatter marks are less critical. These tiny curls that run cross grain an inch or two apart are found in most floors, if you look closely enough. They are more common with sheet-fed drum sanders, especially if you load the paper too tight or too loose. Chatter marks can be minimized or eliminated on most floors by a thorough screening with progressively finer grits.

If you've missed setting a few nails, you may decide to stop the sander and set them as they shine up. You will

hear them strike the paper. If you keep sanding, you will either crease the paper, causing long raised lines to appear in the surface running in the same direction that you're sanding, or you'll rip the paper, causing it to explode out of the machine. When this happens, you'll think the world is coming to an end. You'll be cleaning bits of paper and abrasive particles out of the machine and your floor for a while. In the worst cases, the rubber sleeve on the drum will be damaged, and you'll owe the rental agency for a replacement.

The drum sander can't get closer than about 2 in. to 6 in. of the wall. That's what the edger is for. The edger works a little differently from the drum sander. It cuts more aggressively on the right side of the disc, so it should be moved across the floor from the left to the right, as shown in Figure 36. The usual pattern is a semicircular motion. But there are few other motions, too, some of which are shown in Figure 36.

There are two basic moves you can make with the edger: forward and back, and left to right. Combinations of these result in various patterns, like the zigzag pattern, for sanding parallel to wall lines and large areas and the hoop pattern, a horseshoe-shaped move with the apex of the arc along the wall line. When sanding where flooring

Figure 36 **Sanding with the Edger**

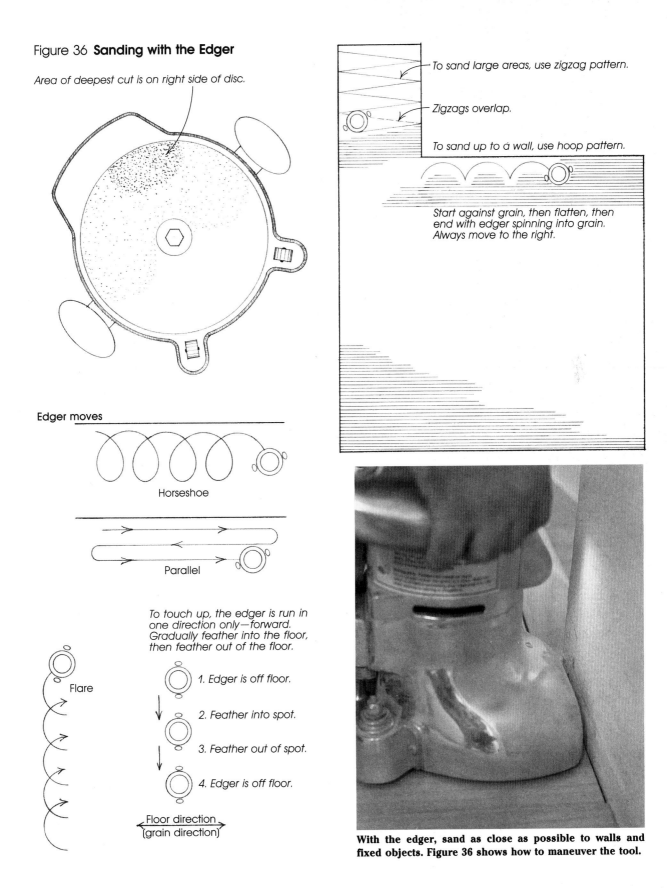

Area of deepest cut is on right side of disc.

To sand large areas, use zigzag pattern.

Zigzags overlap.

To sand up to a wall, use hoop pattern.

Start against grain, then flatten, then end with edger spinning into grain. Always move to the right.

Edger moves

Horseshoe

Parallel

Flare

To touch up, the edger is run in one direction only—forward. Gradually feather into the floor, then feather out of the floor.

1. Edger is off floor.

2. Feather into spot.

3. Feather out of spot.

4. Edger is off floor.

Floor direction
(grain direction)

With the edger, sand as close as possible to walls and fixed objects. Figure 36 shows how to maneuver the tool.

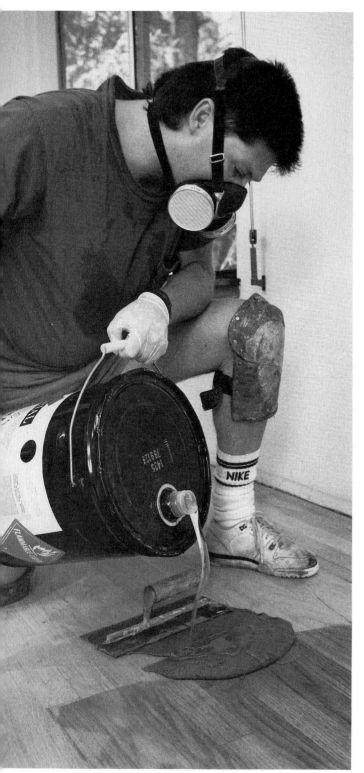

runs under the wall, I use a twist maneuver, in which the edger starts out cross grain to strips or planks, then curves up and out to the right to end up parallel with the grain. Each succeeding pass overlaps the previous one.

One other maneuver I use is called the touchup. You start by lightly feathering the cutting edge into the floor parallel to the grain just to the left and below the spot you want to remove. As you move toward the spot, allow the full weight of the machine to bear on the floor. Once you're past the spot, begin lifting the machine until the paper is off the floor. Just remember to keep the machine moving at all times (Figure 36 on p. 117).

Every sanding machine leaves some kind of marks behind; the trick is to make the marks less and less obvious with finer grits, feathering one sanded area into the next. Feathering with the edger is done by varying grits sizes and cutting depth. Rather than mess with the wheel adjustments for changing the cutting depth, I add or remove sanding discs when I change grits. I usually have only one or two discs on the spinner when roughing. When I switch to medium grit, I like to expand the area in which the paper touches the floor to help smooth out the edger marks.

To do this, I add another disc or two to the spinner plate. This gives the paper a larger footprint on the floor, from 11 o'clock to 2 o'clock on the spinner. For the finest grits, I might run three or four discs, for a coverage between 10 o'clock and 3 o'clock on the wheel. This is the widest area of contact and gives the best results for keeping the floor flat and for smoothing swirl marks.

Filling and medium sanding

Professional floor mechanics argue about a lot of things, but most agree that sanding starts with coarse grits and progresses to the finer papers. As I explained earlier, however, they disagree on the order of events. Some mechanics like to trowel filler once after roughing, then not fill again until between coats. Others insist that spot filling is the only way to go. I like to fill once after rough sanding and spot fill again after medium sanding or between coats of finish, as necessary.

The filler itself can be a commercial product that you mix yourself or a preblended product such as Zar Wood Patch, Goop-On or Famo-Wood. These ready-mixed products are color matched to the species and are simply forced into the cracks and holes with a putty-knife. Once dried, they are sanded flush. They are sold in one-gallon pails, which is the minimum amount you should buy for even a small floor. Of the lacquer-based products, I prefer Wood Doe Base. It's mixed with sawdust right on the floor until it's the consistency of melted butter. I'm gradually switching my allegiance to a latex (water-based) product, Wood Stuff. It can be troweled on or spot filled and does have to be mixed with wood dust. It has no nasty fumes and is not flammable like most other fillers.

Minor cracks and gaps are filled with a lacquer-based product mixed with fine sawdust (above). The filler is troweled over the entire floor and allowed to dry before being resanded (facing page).

Sweep or vacuum the floor after rough sanding before filling. Use a trowel or putty knife to move the blob around the floor to fill cracks, nail holes and knots, all at once. Of course, in order to use Wood Doe Base, you need fine sanding dust (which you'll make in abundance when the floor is sanded). If you're filling after rough sanding though, you won't have any fine dust, so you're better off using a premixed product. Odd as it may sound, I save my fine dust to make putty on upcoming jobs.

Make a good-sized dollop of the stuff and start troweling it around, working from one of the corners toward the center of the room. The filler will settle into the large cracks on its own but may need a little help to get into the fine cracks. Don't worry if you miss a few spots. There will be opportunity later for a second coat of filler. While filling, watch for raised edges that seem to catch the trowel or collect heavier amounts of filler. These indicate low or high spots in the floor that you've missed. Rather than go on to a finer paper, sand again with coarse grit, concentrating on the spots you've missed. Refill the floor by troweling or spot filling. Be sure to remove all excess putty off the floor's surface. Clumps of dried filler will not only gum up sandpaper but also tilt the drum of the big machine, causing nasty gouges.

Lacquer-based fillers or a fast-drying latex filler like Wood Stuff will dry and be ready for sanding in an hour or two. Medium sanding should be done with 80-grit or coarser paper. Use the same pattern and feed rate as for rough sanding, taking care to flatten any spots where there's excess filler. Continue the sanding with the edger, loading the machine with extra discs to expand its footprint, as described on p. 118. Once again, sweep and vacuum, then inspect the floor carefully for any open cracks. These should be spot filled and sanded again.

Final sanding

Finish sand with 100-grit to 120-grit paper, preferably garnet (you can use silicon carbide if that's what you happen to have). Follow the same pattern and try to remove any swirls the coarser paper may have left. When the floor has been completely drum-sanded and edge-sanded with the finest paper, scrape the corners and edges where neither of these machines could reach. Use a common paint scraper whose edge has been sharpened with a file or stone. What you'll be doing here is blending into the floor the high spots that the edge sander couldn't get to.

Where possible, scrape with the grain; in tight spots where the scraper just won't fit, scrape at a 45° angle. Finish by hand sanding those places you scraped, so the stain or finish won't take differently there.

You'll also have to do a little hand sanding around the edges of the floor as well as spot sanding where the drum sander or edger may have left swirls. Sand with the grain, using the same grit or one a little coarser than the one you used for the final sanding. I strongly recommend hand sanding all areas where you used the edger before screening. If you come across any cracks, I don't recommend filling them until after the first coat of finish is applied. Floor fillers are very difficult to smooth with hand sanding alone. Just before finishing (or staining), use a buffer to screen the floor to at least 100 grit.

As shown in the photo on the facing page (and in the videotape) the screenback is loosely attached to the pad on the buffer. A once-over with the screenback is usually enough. Once you're satisfied with the floor, sweep and vacuum it carefully, and you're ready to begin finishing.

If you happen to be sanding a parquet or pattern floor, follow the same order of events as described above. However, use the sanding pattern described in Figure 37 and finish with 150-grit paper if available. Follow by screening with a fine-grit screen (up to 180 grit) to remove the inevitable crossgrain scratching.

To touch up the floor or smooth areas that are not accessible to the edger, use a sharp scraper (left) and then sand by hand (below).

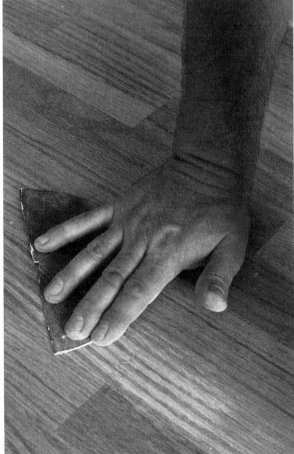

Selecting a finish

Now that the floor is filled and sanded, you're ready for the home stretch—finishing. People are always asking me, "What's the best floor-finishing product?" I always tell them that there is no best product, that the right finish for any floor depends on your needs, experiences and financial constraints as well as on the kind of traffic and spilled substances the floor will have to bear. I like acid-curing Swedish finishes because they're durable and reliable, but they would not be the best choice for most non-professionals. Some floor mechanics swear by moisture-cured urethanes, others prefer oil-modified urethanes, and there are some who like using natural oils or waxes. Penetrating oils, varnishes and shellacs are also options. Finally, water-based finishes are becoming more popular. I'll describe the pros and cons of each type of finish so that you can decide for yourself.

I have avoided mentioning specific brand names below for several reasons. Many products are available only in certain regions of the country, and, because of air-quality regulations, some manufacturers distribute differently formulated products under the same name in different parts of the country. Also, because there are so many changes taking place in the wood-finishing industry, new products (especially water-based products) are being introduced all the time. For the best information on which products may be available to you, check the list of manufacturers under "Stains, waxes and finishes" in the Resource Guide (see p. 135). Write or call them for the names of products and local distributors.

Many, if not most, floor-finishing products contain toxic chemicals and solvents that can be harmful to users and to the environment (see the sidebar on p. 122). So whichever finishing product you choose, it is absolutely essential that you pay close attention to the safety precautions on the label. You may want to contact the manufacturer or retailer of the product to receive a copy of the manufacturer's Material Safety Data Sheet (MSDS), which contains helpful information on the hazardous chemicals contained in the product and the precautions you should take in applying it.

Before the finish is applied and after the first coat, go over the floor with a buffer and screenback. Dust from the buffer makes excellent filler stock.

Figure 37
Sanding a Parquet Floor

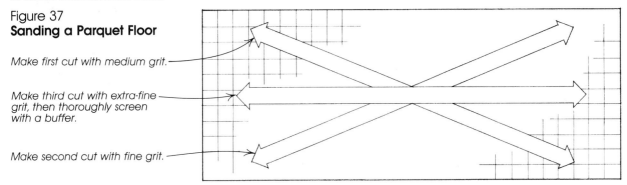

Make first cut with medium grit.

Make third cut with extra-fine grit, then thoroughly screen with a buffer.

Make second cut with fine grit.

Floor finishes and the environment

The work you are doing to give your floors a nice, natural appearance may be doing some nasty, unnatural things to the environment. Like paints, floor finishes contain four general types of ingredients: pigments, which are small, solid particles that give color or hiding ability; resins or polymers, which hold the pigment in the coating; solvents or diluents, which are liquids in which the resins and pigments are dissolved or suspended;

and additives. The solvents in solvent-based finishes are composed of hydrocarbons and other volatile organic compounds (VOCs) that, when released into the atmosphere during the curing process, combine with oxygen and sunlight to create low-level ozone (a principal component of smog).

Ambient air quality standards set by the Environmental Protection Agency (EPA) recommend a maximum

allowable level of VOCs in floor finishes of 350 grams per liter. Many states and localities have passed laws that are even tougher than the EPA recommendations. These standards and laws have affected most of the solvent-based and many of the water-based finishes, and many manufacturers have begun reformulating or modifying their products.

When I'm finishing a floor, I tell clients to leave the premises at least until the finish has had time to dry. Pregnant women, infants, elderly people, people with respiratory ailments or heart conditions, pets and sensitive plants should stay off the premises at least overnight. But these are minimal recommendations. Some finishes, especially acid-curing Swedish and the moisture-cured and oil-modified urethanes, smell so bad that they can literally force you out of your house. And I have found that some people are sensitive to the water-based finishes, even though they have much less of an odor. So you might want to play it safe and simply plan on staying out of the house for 24 to 48 hours after the finish has been applied. If you use one of the finishes that contain formaldehyde, you should understand that formaldehyde may continue off-gassing for weeks or even months after application.

When using solvent-based finishes, all pilot lights, stoves, electric motors and other ignition sources should be turned off. When applying any finish, be sure to wear an appropriate NIOSH/MSHA-approved respirator, chemical goggles and rubber gloves. Specific products may require even more stringent precautions.

Urethanes. Moisture-cured, oil-modified and water-based urethanes are among the most popular floor finishes available today. They are all convertible finishes, which means that they cure by a process called polymer cross-linking. As the finish dries, the polymers cross-link to form a tight matrix. Once polymerized, the coating provides a tough, moisture-resistant film. Almost all coatings used in the wood-floor trade fall into this category. Urethanes are widely available in various brands, degrees of gloss and price ranges.

Since urethanes, along with acid-curing Swedish finishes and the new water-based epoxies, have a greater ability to cross-link than other convertible finishes, they cure to a very hard film that is relatively impermeable to moisture. They are a good choice in high-traffic areas where water may be a transient problem but where the ambient moisture level doesn't change much—kitchens,

dining rooms, living rooms, foyers and bathrooms, for example. Urethanes are long-term finishes, but some yellow with age, especially if exposed to direct sunlight. In sunny rooms, a finish that contains an ultraviolet inhibitor will last longer, especially if you're not staining the floor. Ask your supplier which brands contain inhibitors.

Gloss selection is a matter of personal preference. I think high-gloss urethanes look too much like a thick coating of plastic, so I prefer to use satin or low-gloss finishes. High-gloss coatings are marginally harder than their low-gloss counterparts because the dulling agents added to knock down the gloss make the cured film softer. What really makes a high-gloss finish look worn, however, is the constant abrading in high-traffic areas. Sighting the floor in oblique lighting conditions will make worn spots stand out.

Repairing moisture-cured and water-based urethanes is difficult because fresh urethane doesn't always adhere well to an old coat. If you need to repair your finish but you're unsure about compatibility, test it first in an inconspicuous spot (such as a closet). Sand the old finish first, to improve the "tooth" for the fresh finish. If you aren't satisfied with the results of the test, then you'll have to sand down to bare wood and start over again.

Moisture-cured urethanes react with the humidity in the air to dry. They dry more rapidly in moist environments. They form the hardest wearing surface of any finish I know, but I've found that significant shifts in humidity while curing will cause inconsistent drying that can lead to blistering or other defects. Moisture-cured urethanes are extremely flammable, difficult to apply, contain high levels of volatile organic compounds (VOCs) and are best left to the professional finisher. They are available only in glossy finishes.

Oil-modified urethanes, or, technically speaking, urethane-modified oils, are quite popular as a residential finish. What many manufacturers and floor mechanics call polyurethane is really oil-modified urethane. This is the type of urethane you are almost certain to find in your local retail store. It is easier to apply and repair than

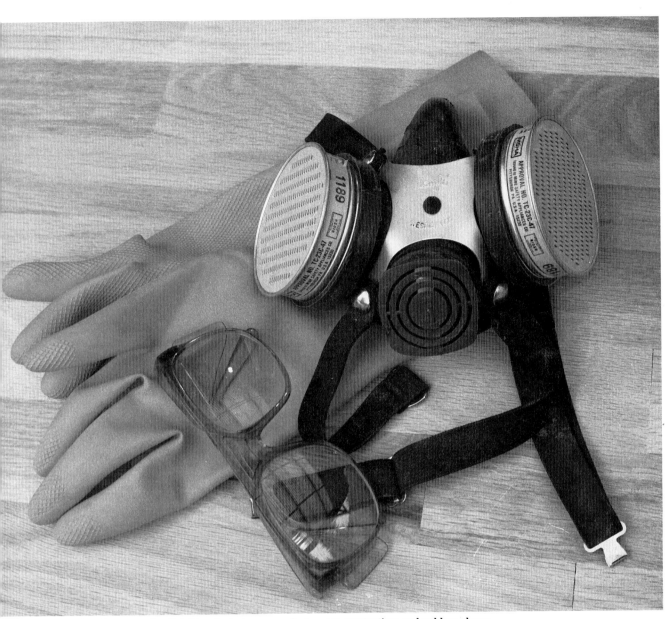

Proper safety gear for finishing includes a respirator, eye protection and rubber gloves.

moisture-cured urethane and acid-curing Swedish finish, although not as easy as oil or wax. It is fast drying but slow to cure and requires sanding between coats. Oil-modified urethane also has a high VOC level, although not as high as other products. It is available in glossy and satin finishes.

Water-based (water-borne) finishes are becoming a very popular product, especially for the do-it-yourselfer. Rather than being suspended primarily in volatile solvents, the solids in these products are suspended mostly in water. Water-based coatings for floors are usually combinations of urethane and acrylic, generally with some type of cata-

lyst mixed into the coating just before application. (Caution: many catalysts are severe skin irritants.) As a general rule, the higher the percentage of urethane, the more expensive and durable the coating will be.

Water-based finishes are applied similarly to solvent-based finishes but generally require more coats to achieve a comparable film thickness. They generally have the color and consistency of nonfat milk, but they dry clear, which makes applying subsequent coats easier because you can see what you've covered. Unlike most solvent-based coatings, most water-based finishes do little to change the color of the wood.

The first coat of water-based urethane raises the grain of the raw wood, which must then be sanded or screened smooth—but take care not to sand through into the wood or you'll only end up raising the grain again with the second coat. Though some may hesitate to apply a water-based product to their bare wood floors, when properly applied very little water is applied per square foot, and a thin coat promotes rapid water evaporation. Water-based finishes are much less noxious than solvent-based finishes, but they still contain VOCs. The absence of offensive odors in most water-based products creates a false sense of security among unwitting users. Many toxic, yet commonly used compounds in coating products have little or no odor. I strongly recommend that you use proper lung, eye and skin protection with water-based finishes.

Oil finishes. Natural oils, such as linseed and tung, are rarely used in their pure state, but they are considered convertible coatings since they eventually cross-link. Several coats of linseed or tung oil will build an abrasion-resistant surface. Most penetrating-oil sealers/finishes are combinations of highly modified natural oils with additives to improve hardness and drying. Oil finishes are generally easy to apply and repair (just brush or rub on another coat), but they are smelly and can take weeks or even months to cure fully. Meanwhile, the surface will collect dust and, when walked on, a film will adhere to shoes and be tracked onto adjacent floors. Also, linseed oil darkens over time. Adding wax to an oil-finished floor will give better protection against spills and abrasion, but periodically you will have to remove it and rewax.

Acid-curing Swedish finishes. The term "Swedish finish" has come to be applied to a whole variety of floor finishes, mostly because of marketing hype. Most wood-floor professionals I know, however, use the term to refer specifically to the acid-curing finishes, which contain formaldehyde. The Swedish finishes are convertibles cured by the addition of a hardener. Swedish finishes are expensive, but they have a reputation for durability, transparency and elasticity.

Applied right to raw wood, acid-curing Swedish finishes tend to bring out the reddish tones of many species. They also raise the grain a bit, but not nearly as much as a water-based product will. Some grain rise is actually beneficial because it causes the surface pores to open up and absorb the finish, giving better adhesion. The raised grain should be flattened with a screenback, abrasive pad or light hand sanding before a second coat is applied.

Acid-curing Swedish finishes are a popular product among many professional floor mechanics. But their high VOC content and the presence of formaldehyde have caused others to stay away from them. They are probably the most difficult finishes to apply and require a carefully sanded floor. In many parts of the country, these finishes are available only to professionals, and they should be used only by those prepared to follow carefully the safety precautions on the label.

There are water-based Swedish finishes, too. These are quite similar to domestically produced water-based coatings, and they are easier to apply and have less odor than their acid-curing counterparts. They are even more expensive than the pricey acid-curing coatings.

Waxes. Although not as common as they once were, wax finishes are very simple to apply and surprisingly durable. They do require a lot of maintenance and are less impervious to moisture and dirt than most other finishes. One of the biggest drawbacks to wax is that it is particularly slippery when wet. Therefore a wax finish would not be prudent in kitchens, entryways or powder rooms. Before wax is applied, the wood must be sealed with a stain or a grain sealer. Some waxes require frequent touchup but are easier to apply and reapply than their more durable counterparts. Others contain hardening agents to provide a faster build and shorter cure time. I find that ordinary paste wax works best.

Wax is applied with a brush or rag (on hands and knees, unfortunately) and polished to the desired luster with an electric buffer. Eventually, most waxes will yellow and become brittle, at which time the wax will have to be removed and a new coat applied. Old wax can be removed with wax removers or renovators if the floor is quite thin or if you want to maintain the patina of the old wood. But professionals and do-it-yourselfers alike will usually find it easier to sand the wax off the floor with floor-sanding equipment. Though easy to use, inexpensive and fast drying, most wax products do contain significant levels of VOCs.

Varnishes and shellacs. Traditional varnishes, which are made from natural oils, have largely been supplanted by alkyd-resin varnishes. Some varnishes are suitable for floors and are easy to find and use. They are less expensive than acid-curing Swedish finishes and urethane coatings, but also less durable.

In my opinion, the most beautiful wood floor can be achieved with shellac and wax. Shellac can give a depth and natural patina to the wood that is hard to achieve with any other type of finish. But shellac is difficult to maintain as it water spots easily and dissolves on contact with even mild solvents like alcohol.

Applying finish

There's nothing particularly mysterious about applying floor finishes. The single best instruction I can give you is this: Read the instructions! I'll give you some general tips that apply to most finishes, but many finishes have special instructions that must be followed to the letter. Pay special attention to the suggested safety precautions on

Begin brushing finish by working away from the light so you can see missed spots and irregularities.

the label. It's also a good idea to get the Material Safety Data Sheet from the manufacturer or retailer. At the very least, for mixing and applying most floor finishes you should wear a NIOSH/MSHA-approved respirator, impermeable gloves and chemical goggles. You should wear protective clothing to prevent skin contact, and you should ventilate the area as soon as the coating has set to allow vapors to escape. Some products may have other warnings and precautions that should be heeded.

Water-based finishes should be brushed on the floor with a synthetic-bristle brush, foam pad or short-nap applicator. These tools help minimize the amount of finish being applied and provide a more even coating. This is important because applying too much finish to bare wood can damage the floor, causing it to warp and swell. Non-water-based coatings should be applied with a natural-bristle brush or lamb's wool applicator. I like using a 12-in. brush designed for floor work. Oils and the slower-drying types of oil-modified urethanes can be applied with a rag and wiped clean.

For applying nearly all types of finishes, I like to use a deep plastic dishpan that will accommodate the entire length of a 12-in. brush. To make cleanup easier, line the pan with an ordinary plastic garbage bag. Combine finish and hardener right in the pan and mix thoroughly with a wooden paddle. Mix a little more than you think you'll need to complete the first coat; this way you won't run out in the middle of the floor. If two of you are coating and you're making two batches at once, pour the mixture back and forth to get an identical mix. Better yet, mix the coating in one big pan and then pour it into separate containers. If the batches aren't identical, you're likely to see a line where the two finishes meet.

Keep rags and solvents handy so you can clean up minor messes as you go. I like to carry a small piece of sandpaper with me during finish work. It comes in handy to take out sweat drips, dried defects and the like.

First coat. Once the floor has been cleaned and vacuumed, you are ready to begin applying finish. Start in a blind corner and work toward an open corner or a point where you can leave the room without having to cross the wet surface. As much as practical, work away from the light so you can see the wet surface and spot any laps (heavy lines) or holidays (missed spots). In a very large room, it's best to start in the corners and work toward the escape route.

Work from the larger rooms to the smaller ones if you can. When you're working out through a doorway, don't forget to brush behind the door while you still have enough room to reach it. Try to brush with the grain in long, smooth strokes that overlap your previous row slightly (4 in. to 6 in. or so). Move gradually into and away from each stroke, especially with finish or touch-up strokes. Avoid letting the bristles of the brush flip up as you finish your stroke.

Cover as much as possible with each stroke, and work toward rather than away from the wet edge. Don't allow the lap to dry, or there will be a noticeable lap mark in the finish. As you brush, check constantly for puddles, lap marks and bits of debris in the finish. Pick out debris with your finger and stash it in a rag. Be particularly alert for body hair or brush bristles. They are easy to miss but embarrassingly obvious when glued to the finished floor. Fortunately, they can usually be removed when the finish is dried with a sharp tool like a razor blade.

Watch out for sweat dropping on the floor. (I usually wear a sweat band to help prevent this.) If you see a sweat drop, lightly sand the wet finish right away and re-coat the area. If you don't, you're likely to leave a white or light spot or a dimple in the finish coat. Waiting until it dries will be too late. Brushing finish into a floor warmed by direct sunlight can dry the finish prematurely, causing it to show more lap marks. Cover the windows, or at least cover the affected section of floor, with a tarp until just before you finish it.

When working down long hallways where the grain runs the short dimension, I will often coat 4 in. to 6 in. out into the floor along each wall line within my reach, then coat the middle section, feathering into the still wet finish on both sides of the hall as I back up.

Continue applying finish until the entire surface of the floor is coated. Again, check for any holidays, and touch up any areas that need it. Most types of finish can be emptied into an airtight container and used again, but check with the manufacturer or supplier before doing this. Don't mix it with another batch unless you're using a premixed product, and definitely don't pour it back into the fresh can. If you're disposing of the finish, let it harden first; then it can usually go to the landfill. Liquid finish and solvents should be disposed of by a toxic-waste disposer or at a landfill that is approved for such materials.

With the room sealed off, allow the finish to dry to the touch. Then let the house air out. Read the directions for guidelines as to when to apply the second coat. Many finishes can be recoated once the first coat is dry to the touch, although allowing a little extra time to cure can be beneficial. If you're uncertain about the floor's readiness for a second coat, test it. Lightly press your thumb into the finish in an inconspicuous spot. If you leave a thumbprint, wait another few hours before recoating.

Second coat. Most finishes require that the first coat be smoothed with an abrasive pad, screen or hand sanding before recoating. The idea is to smooth the surface without sanding through the finish. This process will flatten the raised grain and remove debris that may have lodged in the coating when it was still wet. It also can remove thick finish lines such as drips or laps. Finally, it provides "tooth" for the next coat of finish to grab onto the previously applied coating. Once this is done, vacuum the entire floor carefully.

Brush in broad, sweeping motions, then smooth the wet finish with the grain.

Once the finish has dried, minor blemishes can be filled with colored putty. Put a different color on each finger to match boards of different colors.

Before you begin applying the second coat, be sure to read the label of the product you are using and follow the manufacturer's recommendations. Generally, you will apply the second coat just like the first. Use the knowledge you gained on the first coat, and take extra care to avoid lap marks, puddles and embedded debris. Once the finish has dried, inspect carefully for any blemishes. If small, these can be filled with colored putty (see the photo at left). If this is the final coat, it will be your last chance to get it right, although you can usually touch up lap lines, holidays and other finish blemishes with steel wool, a scraper or razor blade or a light buffing.

Maintaining the finish

The care of your floor will depend on the type of finish you used. Most types of urethanes and Swedish finishes can be damp-mopped lightly with a mixture of white vinegar and water (one cup of vinegar per gallon of water) or other mild cleaning solution. Regular cleaning can be done with a vacuum or untreated dust mop. Never use oil soaps, lemon oil, sprays, liquid waxes or any other solutions without first checking with your finish manufacturer or supplier.

If you have an oil or wax finish, you can usually safely use a treated dust mop or vacuum for regular cleaning. I do not recommend the use of a damp mop on waxed or oiled floors.

One final tip: Great care should be taken when placing potted plants on your new floor. Overflow bowls and clay pots account for nearly half the water damage I see in wood flooring. I suggest placing at least ½ in. of dense cork, available at most hardware stores, between potted plants and wood flooring.

Furniture with sharp edges will damage a freshly cured finish. Check all of your furniture and install rubber or plastic glides, if necessary.

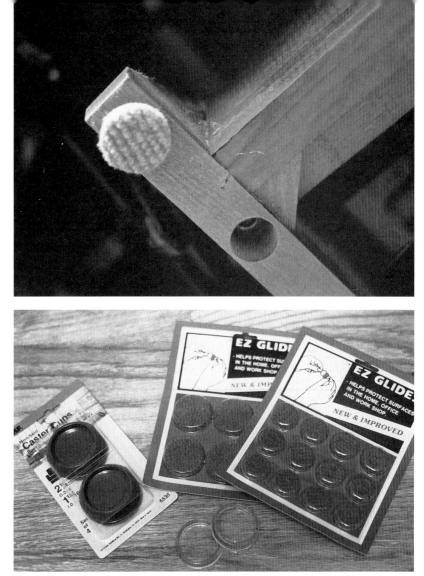

Tips on Staining a Floor

Although I'm usually quite happy with the natural color a clear finish imparts to a wood floor, some of my clients ask me to stain their floors. This is often the case when the species they've selected doesn't quite measure up to their expectations. I always let them know, however, that the stain is the weak link in the finish operation. I've found that clear-finished floors are more durable than their stained counterparts, chiefly because you never know when a stain will create problems in the finish coats.

Traditionally, stains were also used as a base coat and to seal the wood grains of porous species like oak or ash, resulting in a smoother final finish. These days finishes don't usually require sealers but stains are still useful, especially if you want to even out undesirable color variations. Usually, a coat of stain can substitute for the first coat of finish.

Stains can be grouped according to two characteristics: the tinting medium and the carrying medium, or vehicle. Stains generally get their color from dyes, pigments or a combination of the two. In dye stains, the coloring is dissolved in the vehicle. The dye actually colors the wood grain and is absorbed into it. With pigmented stains, the pigment is dispersed and held in suspension so the pigments aren't absorbed and don't actually color the wood grain. They also don't adhere as well as dyes, and their handling is more involved. Since there's less absorption and adhesion, finishes applied over pigment stains aren't as durable as those applied over dye stains.

Dye stains are generally earth tones like reds, yellows, blues and browns. They are fairly translucent, enhancing rather than obscuring the grain of the wood. Pigment colors are usually very light or very dark colors like whites, pastels, greys and blacks. These do hide the wood grain somewhat but provide more uniformity between pieces of different color.

Vehicles for stains are of three general types: water based, fast dry and oil based. Water-based stains set up much more rapidly than oil-based products, and they meet restrictive laws on air pollution. They also have very little odor, but tend to raise the grain more than oil-based stains do. Fast-dry stains are similar to oil-based stains, but incorporate driers and other components to expedite curing. Oil-based stains are the traditional choice for floors and are still the most widely used. Generally speaking, because they dry slowly, oil-based stains are easier to apply and are less likely to "bleed back" into surface coats. Bleed back occurs when solvents contained in finish products eat away at the undried stains, sometimes causing voids or variations in color.

Whatever type of stain you use, make sure it's compatible with the finish you'll be applying and that it's dry before you apply the finish. Sometimes this is easier said than done, since some finishes don't always have this information on the label. Many old-timers say that as long as you let the stain dry thoroughly, any kind of finish is compatible. But if you have any doubts at all, call the finish manufacturer just to be safe.

Selecting a color. The best time to select a stain is during rough sanding. The basic color can be decided well in advance, but leave the final decision until you begin sanding. Lighting, wall and ceiling colors, furniture and cabinet colors and the flooring itself will vary from house to house, so it's best to pick the color that will actually go on the wood in that room.

Prepare a test area on your floor by sanding a small spot with the same grits and screens you'll use on the rest of the floor. Clean the test area, then apply the stain with rags or a brush. Wipe off the excess, and let the stain dry for several hours or overnight. If you're contemplating different shades,

apply the variations side by side. The finish will, of course, change the appearance of the stain slightly. Although it's not always practical to finish the test area, some mechanics insist on doing so, especially if they suspect the color will be difficult to control. If you go this route, let the finish dry before assessing the result. After you've decided on a color, rough sand the test area to clean it up and proceed with sanding the rest of the floor.

Once you've settled on a color, immediately mix a sufficient amount to do the entire floor area. Stain coverage varies, so refer to the product's label. Expect 15% to 25% less coverage when staining top-nailed floors, parquet, soft woods and quartersawn woods, which absorb more stain. To speed drying, I mix one tablespoon of Japan drier into each gallon of solvent-based stain used. Make absolutely certain you've got enough stain to do the entire floor. Running out near the end of the job means you'll have to restain the entire floor, since matching two lots of stain is difficult, if not impossible. Some finishers "box" different containers of the same color by pouring them from can to can, thereby evening any minor color variations.

I apply a bit of the newly mixed solution to the test area to make sure I've reproduced the color correctly. I then pour the newly mixed solution into an airtight container and store it out of direct sunlight.

Prepare for staining by vacuuming the floor thoroughly with a wide, stiff brush attachment. I try to carry the vacuum during this step rather than rolling it, so the machine's wheels won't leave marks. Walk on the floor only with clean, soft-soled shoes or stocking feet. Near the door, I like to leave a clean towel dampened with a solvent compatible with the stain. I use it to clean my shoes each time I go back into the room. Use a crevice tool to clean dust out of corners, on top of any base molding and around heating and cooling ducts. It's a good idea to stuff newspaper into ducts to keep them from blowing dust on fresh stain or finish.

I recommend masking off any masonry area adjacent to the floor to prevent tiny bits of sand from falling onto the floor during finishing. Masking walls, woodwork, cabinets, carpet or other adjacent areas is not a bad idea either, since stain splashed on these will be difficult to remove. Penetrating stains can wick through masking tape, so seal any raw wood trim that might be near the floor line before you stain next to it.

Applying stains. Staining is best done by two people, one applying, the other wiping. Before beginning, go over in your mind exactly where you'll start and finish and decide what direction you'll move. As with finishing, try to work away from the light and toward an escape route. Hand rubbing and wiping with rags is probably the most common method of applying stains, but thin-bodied materials and fast-drying stains can be brushed on. Rags for staining need to be absorbent and lint free, such as lint-free cotton waste sold by auto-parts stores or finishing suppliers. Synthetic fabrics don't work very well.

For staining, use a container with a large opening, like a plastic dishpan lined with a plastic garbage bag. Don't fill the container, or the stain will slop onto the floor and you won't have room to squeeze soaked rags. Mix the stain well, both in the can and occasionally during application. Heavy pigment stains require frequent agitation to keep the pigments from settling and affecting the color.

To begin, wet a clean rag with stain, then wring it out. Apply the stain in a half-moon, circular motion. If you're brushing, brush against the grain first, then with the grain. The idea is to rub the stain throughly into the grain. Apply only as much stain as can be comfortably reached and wiped by your assistant before it becomes too tacky to remove. In hot weather, stain smaller areas, and don't let the stain remain on the floor for more than a few minutes. Wipe it off thoroughly with a clean rag. Staining too large an area will result

in uneven wiping and drying. Try to cut each new stain line along a strip or plank, with the grain.

If you're working with parquet or a patterned floor, try to keep stain lines aligned with a board or pattern change. Work quickly in areas that have to be stained cross grain, because wiping in a different direction will cause the stain to be absorbed at a different rate. If necessary to achieve better blending, keep a wet stain line or overlap stain lines to rewet sections already wiped. Take care though, or you risk uneven color absorption. The wiper should have handy a large plastic garbage bag for stashing soiled staining rags.

When you are finished applying the stain, close up the bag and store it outside until the rags can be washed out with water or disposed of. Don't store the rags inside! Rags soaked with oil-based stains are susceptible to spontaneous combustion.

Improving penetration. Very tight-grained woods, beech and maple for example, are sometimes reluctant to absorb stain evenly. Adding solvents to the stain will improve penetration, and applying two or three thinned-down coats is better than one thick coat. Make sure the solvent is compatible with the stain, and experiment on a scrap before committing to the floor. If you do thin, make all the coats of consistent viscosity and mix them together for a good color match.

Some finishers like to recoat a floor over and over with a heavy pigment stain to get more opacity. This is not a good idea. The more stain you apply, the longer it will take to dry and cure, and the less adhesion your finish will have.

Some old-timers say you can improve stain penetration by a process called burnishing. Essentially, burnishing involves heating up the surface with friction. Burnishing dry or nearly dry stain evaporates the remaining solvents and promotes an even-looking surface. It will also tend to remove gummy or thick spots in the stain that might have resulted from puddling or uneven absorption. If you burnish before staining, you'll seal the floor and make it harder for the stain to penetrate.

Here's how burnishing is done. Load a fine-grit paper onto the drum sander, or use the paper you just finished sanding with. Next, remove as much of the abrasive grit as possible by lifing the front shroud and holding another piece of paper against the running belt. Be very careful. The moving belt is liable to grab the loose paper, so keep your hands as far from the drum as possible. Once you've removed most of the abrasive particles from the belt, run the sander over the floor just as though finish sanding, only more quickly. Don't stop at any point. Since there's not enough abrasive to cut, the belt will mainly develop heat, burnishing and smoothing the surface.

Some exotic woods (teak, for example) and domestic woods like pitch pine contain oils that keep stain from penetrating evenly. One method of dealing with this is called "raking." In raking a floor, you simply dissolve the surface oils with the appropriate solvent, allowing the stain to penetrate the wood's pores more evenly.

You can rake a floor with any of several solvents—lacquer thinner, mineral spirits, alcohol or even water. Don't apply too much water, however, or the floor may cup and warp. As when using any volatile solvent, wear appropriate safety gear, extinguish pilot lights and isolate spark sources. Apply the solvent with a sponge, mop or brush, rub it in vigorously, then remove it with clean rags or towels. Once the floor is dry, stain it immediately before the oils have a chance to seep back to the surface.

One last-ditch tactic to improve penetration is to sand with a coarser grit and skip the screening. Stop the sanding at 80 grit or 100 grit. Be careful, however, because most stains emphasize crossgrain sander marks. If you go this route, hand sand very carefully in any areas where you used the edger and at least 4 in. to 6 in. into the main part of the floor covered by the drum sander.

Before applying any finish coats, be certain your stain is thoroughly dry. You can usually tell by the lack of a solvent smell, but you can also test for dryness by vigorously rubbing various sections of the floor with a clean white towel. If the towel comes away clean, you're ready to finish.

Resource Guide

Equipment

Abrasives

Johnson Abrasives
20 Fitzgerald Drive
Jaffrey, NH 03452
(800) 642-4265

Norton Company
1 New Bond St.
P.O. Box 15008
Worcester, MA 01615
(508) 795-5000

Pro-Cut Products, Inc.
10901 Alder Circle
P.O. Box 550340
Dallas, TX 75355
(800) 527-1403

3-M Contractor Products
Building 225-4S-08, 3M Center
St. Paul, MN 55144
(612) 733-5454

Virginia Abrasives
2851 Service Rd.
Petersburg, VA 23805
(800) 446-1805

Countersinks and drill bits

W. L. Fuller, Inc.
P.O. Box 8767
Warwick, RI 02888
(401) 467-2900

Jamb saws

Crain Cutter Company, Inc.
P.O. Box 361450
Milpitas, CA 95035
(800) 538-7810

Moisture meters

Delmhorst
51 Indian Lane East
Towaco, NJ 07082
(800) 222-0638

Lignomat GmbH
Rotweg 21
D-7148 Remseck 3 (Hochberg)
West Germany
(0 71 46) 50 31

Nailers and fasteners

Porta-Nails, Inc. (Porta-Nailer)
P.O. Box 1257
Wilmington, NC 28402
(919) 762-6334

Primatech, Inc.
990 Ste-Thérèse
Quebec, Quebec, Canada G1N 1S9
(418) 682-2127

Senco Products
P.O. Box 216
Milford, OH 45150
(800) 543-4596

Stanley-Bostich
Feltloc Lane
E. Greenwich, RI 02818
(800) 556-6696

Sanders

Clark Industries, Inc.
101 S. Hanley
St. Louis, MO 63105
(314) 721-7255

Essex-Silverline Corporation
P.O. Box 40
Dracut, MA 01826
(800) 451-5560

Floorco
21 Research Road
Toronto, Ontario, Canada M4G 2G7
(416) 421-7651

Galaxy Electric
1 & 1A Musgrave St.
Toronto, Ontario, Canada M4E 2H3
(416) 691-4315

Flooring

Unfinished oak flooring

B. A. Mullican Lumber and Mfg.
Company
P.O. Box 249
Vonore, TN 37885
(615) 884-6111

DeSoto Hardwood Flooring
Company
P.O. Box 40895
Memphis, TN 38174
(901) 774-9672

Dixon Lumber Company
P.O. Box 907
Galax, VA 23433
(703) 236-2941

McMinnville Manufacturing
P.O. Box 151
McMinnville, TN 37110
(615) 473-2131

Miller & Company, Inc.
P. O. Box 779
Selma, AL 36701
(205) 874-8271

Missouri Hardwood Flooring
Company
114 N. Gay Ave.
St. Louis, MO 63105
(314) 727-2267

Oregon Lumber Company
(end-grain block flooring)
P.O. Box 711
Lake Oswego, OR 97034
(800) 824-5671

Peace Flooring Company, Inc.
(parquet)
P.O. Box 87
Magnolia, AR 71753
(501) 234-2310

Stuart Flooring Corporation
P.O. Box 947
Stuart, VA 24171
(703) 694-4547

Unfinished and prefinished oak flooring

Bruce Hardwood Floors
Triangle Pacific Corporation
16803 Dallas Parkway
Dallas, TX 75248
(214) 931-3000

Tarkett Hardwood Floors
North American Division
P.O. Box 300
Johnson City, TN 37605
(615) 928-3122

Memphis Hardwood Flooring
Company (Chickasaw)
1551 N. Thomas St.
Memphis, TN 38107
(901) 526-7306

Prefinished and laminated oak flooring

Anderson Hardwood Floors
P.O. Box 1155
Clinton, SC 29325
(803) 833-6250

Hartco/Tibbals Flooring Company
300 S. Main St.
Oneida, TN 37841
(615) 569-8526

Unfinished maple flooring

Action Floor Systems, Inc.
P.O. Box 469
Mercer, WI 54547
(715) 476-3512

AGA Corporation
P.O. Box 246
Amasa, MI 49903
(906) 822-7311

Horner
P.O. Box 380
Dollar Bay, MI 49922
(906) 482-1180

Robbins, Inc.
4777 Eastern Ave.
Cincinnati, OH 45226
(513) 871-8988

Unfinished pine and fir flooring

E. T. Moore, Jr. Company
3100 N. Hopkins Rd., Suite 101
Richmond, VA 23224
(804) 231-1823

The Joinery Company
P.O. Box 518
Tarboro, NC 27886
(919) 823-3306

Mountain Lumber Company
P.O. Box 289
Ruckersville, VA 22968
(804) 985-3646

Oregon Lumber Company. *See* "Unfinished oak flooring."

Robinson Lumber Company, Inc.
4700 Hwy. 80 East, Suite 5
Savannah, GA 31410
(912) 897-0020

Walnut, cherry, hickory, ash and other unusual domestic flooring

Aged Woods, Inc.
147 W. Philadelphia St.
York, PA 17403
(800) 233-9307

Frank Purcell Walnut Lumber Co.
P.O. Box 5115
Kansas City, KS 66119
(913) 371-3135

Indiana Hardwood Specialists, Inc.
R.R. 5, Box 241
Spencer, IN 47460
(812) 829-4866

Custom parquet, exotic or custom-designed flooring

Bangkok Industries, Inc.
4562 Worth St.
Philadelphia, PA 19124
(215) 537-5800

East Teak Trading Group, Inc.
P.O. Box 322
Kirkland, WA 98083
(800) 537-3369

Exotic Wood Products
P.O. Box 16392
Seattle, WA 98116
(206) 622-6996

Firebird Industries
336 Hord St.
New Orleans, LA 70123
(800) 634-3829

International Hardwood Flooring, Inc.
7400 Edmund St.
Philadelphia, PA 19136
(800) 338-7481

Kentucky Wood Floors
P.O. Box 33276
Louisville, KY 40232
(502) 451-6024

Quality Woods Limited
P.O. Box 205
Lake Hiawatha, NJ 07034
(201) 927-0742

Floating wood flooring systems
Boen Hardwood Flooring, Inc.
Route 5, Box 640
Bassett, VA 24055
(703) 629-3381

Tarkett Hardwood Floors. *See* "Unfinished and prefinished oak flooring."

Kahrs International, Inc.
25057 Viking St.
Hayward, CA 94545
(415) 887-4420

Acrylic-impregnated flooring
The Applied Radiant Energy Corporation (Gammapar)
Venture Drive
Forest Comercial Center
P.O. Box 289
Forest, VA 24551
(804) 525-5252

Hartco/Tibbals Flooring Company. *See* "Prefinished and laminated oak flooring."

PermaGrain Products, Inc.
13 W. 3rd St.
Media, PA 19063
(215) 565-1575

Vinyl-covered wood flooring
ARCO Chemical Company (GenuWood II)
Architectural Products
3801 Westchester Pike
Newtown, PA 19073
(215) 359-2000

Wood vents
ClassicAire Woodvents
7493 SE Overland St.
Portland, OR 97222
(800) 545-8368

Materials

Adhesives
Bostik Construction Products
P.O. Box 8
Huntington Valley, PA 19006
(800) 221-8726

Franklin International
2020 Bruck St.
Columbus, OH 43207
(614) 443-0241

Tec Inc. and H. B Fuller Company
315 S. Hicks Rd.
Palatine, IL 60067
(708) 358-9500

W. W. Henry Company
5608 Soto St.
Huntington Park, CA 90255
(213) 583-4961

Concrete sealers and leveling compounds
Bostik Construction Products. *See* "Adhesives."

Chemique, Inc. (HB-500)
315 N. Washington Ave.
Moorestown, NJ 08057-2408
(609) 235-4161

Franklin International. *See* "Adhesives."

Raeco, Inc. (Raecolith)
915 S. Carstens Place
Seattle, WA 98108
(206) 763-1335

Filling compounds
Beverly Manufacturing (Famowood)
9118 South Main
Los Angeles, CA 90003
(800) 678-3266

Central Valley Chemical (Goop-On)
P.O. Box 188
Sacramento, CA 95801
(916) 383-2304

Color Putty Company, Inc.
121 West 7th St.
Monroe, WI 53566
(608) 325-6033

ECO STREAM Products
Div. of Wood Floor Products, Inc. (Wood Stuff)
20420 142nd St.
Kent, WA 98042
(800) 458-5880

Imperial Paint Company (Wood Doe Base)
2526 N.W. Yeon Ave.
Portland, OR 97210
(503) 228-0207

United Gilsonite Laboratories (Zar Wood Patch)
P.O. Box 70
Scranton, Pa. 18501
(800) 845-5227

Metal strip for inlay
Alaskan Copper & Brass Company
P.O. Box 3546
Seattle, WA 98124
(206) 623-5800

Exotic Wood Products. *See* "Custom parquet, exotic or custom-designed flooring."

Sound-deadening material

Cork Insulation Sales Company, Inc.
1943 1st Ave. South
P.O. Box 3822
Seattle, WA 98134
(206) 622-1094

Tarkett Hardwood Floors (Quiet Core). *See* "Unfinished and prefinished oak flooring."

Stains, waxes and finishes

Absolute Coatings, Inc.
34 Industrial St.
Bronx, NY 10461
(800) 221-8010

W. M. Barr Co.
P.O. Box 1879
Memphis, TN 38101
(800) 238-2672
(901) 775-0100

Basic Coatings
P.O. Box 677
Des Moines, IA 50303
(800) 247-5471
(515) 288-0231

BonaKemi USA, Inc.
5450 Joliet St.
Denver, CO 80239
(303) 371-1411

Casco Nobel
Praestemosevej 2-4
Fredensborg, Denmark DK-3480
45-2-281066

Crawford Laboratories
4165 S. Emerald Ave.
Chicago, IL 60609
(312) 376-7132

Dalys, Inc.
3525 Stone Way North
Seattle, WA 98103
(206) 633-4200

Diamondlac Corp.
12108 Mukilteo Speedway
Lynnwood, WA 98037
(206) 743-9311

Glitsa American
327 S. Kenyon
Seattle, WA 98108
(800) 527-8111
(206) 763-2855

Harco Chemical Coatings, Inc.
208 Dupont St.
Brooklyn, NY 11222
(800) 445-3777
(718) 389-3777

Hillyard Chemical Co.
P.O. Box 909
St. Joseph, MO 64502
(800) 365-1555
(816) 233-1321

Johnson Wax
1525 Howe St.
Racine, WI 53403
(414) 631-4306

McCloskey Corp.
7600 State Rd.
Philadelphia, PA 19136
(215) 624-4400

McGrevor Coatings
1701 Utica Ave.
Brooklyn, NY 11204
(800) 922-9981
(718) 377-0505

Minwax Company, Inc.
15 Mercedes Drive
Montvale, NJ 07645
(800) 526-0495
(201) 391-0253

Pratt & Lambert
P.O. Box 1505
Buffalo, NY 14240
(800) 647-2253
(716) 873-2770

Watco-Dennis Corp.
Rancho Dominguez, CA 90220

Trade associations

Maple Flooring Manufacturers Association (MFMA)
60 Revere Drive, Suite 500
Northbrook, IL 60062
(708) 480-9138

National Oak Flooring Manufacturers Association (NOFMA)
22 North Front St., Suite 660
Memphis, TN 38103
(901) 526-5016

National Wood Flooring Association (NWFA)
11046 Manchester Rd.
St. Louis, MO 63122
(800) 422-4556

Index

Editor	Paul Bertorelli
Designer/layout artist	Ben Kann
Copy/production editor	Ruth Dobsevage
Illustrator	Vince Babak
Art assistants	Jodie A. Delohery, Iliana Koehler
Print production managers	Peggy Dutton, Tom Greco
Typesetter	Nancy Knapp
Indexer	Harriet Hodges
Typeface	ITC Cheltenham Light